LIFE INTERRUPTED
Break the Silence and Heal the Core within You

By Luann Durand

Editor's notes

The names, details and circumstances may have been changed to protect the privacy of those mentioned in this publication.

This publication is not intended as a substitute for the advice of health care professionals.

Cover design: Grant Pignato
Interior design: Grant Pignato
Back Cover design: Luann Durand

LIFE IS BETTER WITH A BRUSH IN YOUR HAND

TABLE OF CONTENTS

INTRODUCTION

On a warm, sunny day, I am sitting under the canopy in my backyard in West Palm Beach, Florida. Banyan Lake, just behind our home, is glimmering in the afternoon sun and birds are joyfully singing in the distance. A breeze wafts softly across my bare shoulders. This is my favorite place for inspiration. As I sit quietly in my wicker chair, legs crossed into a lotus, I begin to go inward. Nature around me calms my heart. It allows me to find patience and creativity. I take in the breathtaking scenery, and inspiration fills my blank canvas with colors. I turn on music to find my perfect rhythm—today it's jazz, and the buttery sound of Steve Tyrell floats whimsically in the air. Vibrant colors flow back and forth, as I paint from my heart. I sit in stillness. I realize that life passes so quickly and yet there is so much to understand in every moment.

Today, I am just shy of fifty-seven and I still feel thirty. Sometimes I have absolutely no idea where the time has gone. However, this moment is a time of reflection; a time for me to acknowledge one of the true purposes life has bestowed upon me: to empower women, and encourage them to use their voice. While that mission has taken many forms, I am honored that today it means writing a book for you, dear reader.

It's true that in any life there are both happy and sad times. Everyone, to some degree, suffers in the wake of what life has fatefully thrown. We tend to live with a picture-perfect idea of how things will pan out. We visualize our life unfolding with ease—whether that means excelling in a career, having a family, or simply being healthy. We are hopeful (to a fault sometimes) and then bam!—life throws a curveball. Things go unplanned. Relationships fail, health is in jeopardy, or worse, trauma occurs. While everyone around you may look as if things are peachy keen, in reality, everyone—at some point—faces what I call an interruption: a chaotic time in life when everything goes haywire.

As you may have guessed, a few interruptions have fallen into my life. In fact, interruptions have been happening nonstop! But, through the darkness and pain, I have discovered a life of peace and joy. I want that for you too. I wrote this book to both share my story, and to inspire you to rewrite yours. If you've had interruptions in your life, I know they can feel like a revolving door: even though they've passed in time, the pain can remain stuck in your soul, reoccurring in your life as illness, toxic relationships, or energetic blocks. They haunt you and stop you from evolving into your best self.

For me, life is like an apple: while the outside is sweet, the rough, gritty center holds the seeds—where all the hope and inspiration for new growth lies. It is with divine intelligence that those seemingly unremarkable seeds are able to produce a giant new tree. In every life, a sweet exterior hides a tough core. Every human possesses the same wisdom the apple does. It's in our hearts, and at the core of each of our interruptions, that holds the strength to persevere. While it may feel daunting or uncomfortable to get to this deeper place, once you do, you are rewarded with life-affirming wisdom. I'm living proof that it's true. If you are courageous enough to get here, a vibrant new life awaits you: a freed spirit, and a revived sense of confidence!

If you choose to get to the core and allow vulnerability to take place, then fear will no longer be a ruling force in your life. You will be set free. So, ask yourself: Are you ready to Break the Silence and Heal the Core Within?

Life Interrupted

CHAPTER 1

SILENCE INTERRUPTED

"All Dis-EASE comes from a state of unforgiveness."
– Louise Hay

THE YEAR IS 1978. I'm standing in front of a bathroom mirror in my parent's home in Greendale, Wisconsin. It's about three o'clock in the afternoon, and I'm applying lipstick. Gazing back at my reflection, I drag the pale pink color across my lips. He should be here any moment. It's February and I don't have to be at the restaurant until the evening. I adjust the white silky frock I picked out, pulling it off my shoulders. The radio sings loudly through the empty house; Donna Summer belts "Bad Girl" over and over to no one.

I shut it off with a dull click. I'm restless. Where is he? I want to see him before I have to spend the rest of the evening showing impatient airport travelers to their tables until two am. I turn sideways and evaluate my stomach in the mirror. With a deep inhale, I pull it in. I can hear his voice in my head. "Chubs," he called me. I tug on my slip that has a mind of its own, not covering what needs to be covered. It's too tight but I'm too anxious to change. I hope I look thin enough.

He was a bad habit of mine, at least my parents thought so, and did my brothers. No one very close to me liked him, which only made me want him more. Always the rebellious one, I was attracted to someone off-limits. My parents didn't like that he was older—almost 30. I was only eighteen and still living in that strange, transient time between childhood and adulthood. I was just as lost as the customers I served, unknowing of the future, sometimes hopeful but mostly astray. He was someone that I chased, senselessly, attracted to his mysteriousness and his illusion of maturity. He had a car and an apartment when I was still in my senior year of high school. None of the boys my age interested me and I wanted a real man. When I watched him bartend late nights at Pipe Organ Pizza, the local restaurant down the street, I felt my pulse quicken. I watched night after night, mesmerized by the way his muscular physique moved to pour the drinks, the way I felt when he finally kissed me…

The doorbell rings and I jump. My heart pounds in my throat as I open the door. As soon as I lay eyes on him, I know he's drunk. He smiles dumbly at me, his eyes looking far away and watery. He pulls me in for a hug and I smell Jack Daniels as I bury my face into the collar of his denim jacket. He forcibly tilts my head back for a kiss and I cringe.

He pushes me through the house, through the back door, and into the bedroom by the garage. I feel sick. It's 3:15 and no one is home. The sky is gray and quiet. No birds are singing in the cool air, no sounds, just stillness and unease. He pulls me towards the bed, his aggression building. Stupid mutterings fall out of lips. Nasty words ring in my ears as he works his arms under my shirt, grabbing and taking. I resist him. I press both my hands into his chest, arms quivering under the weight of him, but he falls on top, smashing my lungs. Like an avalanche, we fall together and I can't breathe.

I close my eyes and I'm alone in my head. I'm telling him to stop but he doesn't. He tears off my clothes before I know what's happened. I smell liquor. Shrieking, I dig my nails into his skin. He is sweating and grunting, eyes looking straight into mine but also so far away, so gone, so alone. I hate him at this moment. Hate burns deeper in my soul then I had even known it could. I am lifeless. My body is no longer my own. In an instant, he takes everything away from me: my innocence and my purity. With fury, he takes me, steals me, and violates me, over and over. He grabs my head and forces it downward. I am screaming in my mind and crying in my heart. It was my first time....

I was eighteen and believed this is what was supposed to happen. I believed this is what people did when they were in love.

CHAPTER 2

TIPPING THE SCALE

"Now I choose to rise above my personality and problems and recognize the magnificence of my being." — Louise Hay

I WAS BORN in 1960, in a quiet, picturesque neighborhood with manicured grass lawns and tree-lined streets. My sister was only thirteen months older than me, and three curious younger brothers followed. My parents raised us in Milwaukee, where we played outside until the streetlights came on. Having survived the Depression, my parents were resilient, industrious, and hardworking. My father worked long hours at a family-owned bakery that sold elegant wedding cakes, cheese torte, bread, and sliced deli meat. Though he possessed great mental fortitude, his physical well-being wavered; he suffered from a blood disorder that made him especially susceptible to illness. Many times, he was hospitalized, and my mom was forced into independence. At times, she feared to raise five young children alone. She was a patient and dutiful mother but even at a young age, I felt her walking on eggshells when it came to my father's health: each time he was sent to the hospital she feared, it may be the last.

Growing up, I was somewhat opposite of my sister. She had bleach blonde hair, fair skin, and light eyes— just like my mother. I had my father's dark Italian skin, chestnut curls, and dark blue eyes. We were the classic tomboy and princess caricatures, with my sister being the latter. We embraced these simple identities as our entrance into the world as females. My sister and I would pose side by side for family photos, tugging and squirming in our coordinated outfits. She was styled in all blue and me in all red, which I resented.

Even early on, I struggled to find myself. I wanted to rebel against my parents when I felt labeled. I begged my mother for a blue outfit next time (it was my favorite color), but I ended up wearing every other color instead, just to shut me up. Any semblance of individuality never came.

Our neighborhood was peaceful and idyllic. Children played on the streets, chasing each other in endless games of tag until the glow of fireflies could be seen through the dusk. We were given modest allowances for chores and when I had a dollar saved, I would walk to the candy store and spend it on jellybeans, chocolate coins, and homemade taffy. I remember the sweet, sticky feeling of my top teeth glued to my bottom ones while walking home on those carefree summer evenings, my saddle shoes smacking the suburban sidewalk with each step.

When I was five, we moved to a much bigger home in Greendale, on the south side of Milwaukee. There, we settled into a dramatic redbrick home with a pool and a circular driveway. My parents were quite the Midwest socialites. Parties happened every weekend in our house, along with the drinks, food, laughs, and calamities they entailed. Our home was always filled with guests and burst at the seams with noise. I made up games to play with my sister, and if we were lucky, we got to taste a little champagne from the bottles that my mother would pop open like rockets exploding into the night sky.

As we grew older and a bit more self-aware, I noticed my sister and me shaping into our unique forms. When I reached age nine, my body was much different than hers. Though we were not so far in age, I was several inches taller, with thick legs that were widening underneath me. My sister was athletic and lean. When her toned legs would dive gracefully into our pool, I began to become aware of our differences.

The nights of parties meant many slices of pizza, followed by many scoops of ice cream, followed by donuts in the morning when my mother was too tired to cook breakfast. I was a child and ate everything handed to me, unaware. It was the '60's, and not only was nearly every subject relating to womanhood off limits, but no effort was extended toward me in any way to educate me about my body. I had no idea about food, calories, exercise, or dieting. Consequently, I gained weight. I felt trapped in a body that didn't feel like mine. I couldn't understand why my sister was living a parallel life to me but having a much different experience, without the shame and loneliness that began to overtake me as I became increasingly aware of my overweight self.

At school, the humiliation of my weight gain magnified. As I progressed through grade school, I felt my breasts beginning to shape under my cardigans and my hips widening without my consent. I was too young to understand what was happening to me.

With every passing week, I gained more weight. I heard other children whispering about me in the hallways, especially boys. At age nine and ten, they were all stick-thin before puberty had arrived. It was humiliating enough to be developing early, but being a girl in a school full of boys made it worse. It was becoming clear that I was chosen to be an early bloomer. Today I see that as beautiful, and I think it makes me special. However, as a ten-year-old, my changing body only caused me complete and utter devastation.

One day during this time, I was running on the playground in a tense game of kickball. We were divided into teams. As I ran from base to base, the boys on the opposite team yelled offensively at me. We were down to the wire, only a few minutes left in recess, and I was about to make a home run for my team. (At least that's what I believed in my mind. In reality, I would be lucky to just reach first base.) Sports had never been a favorite pastime of mine, but I longed to be fit and athletic like my sister. I wanted her lean legs and for the other kids to root for me. As I ran, I felt my legs stomping into the ground, my breasts dangling without the help of a training bra.

The boys watching lost it.

"Too chubby to run!" I heard them scream as I ran past first base.

"Come on fatso, give up!"

Tears welled in my eyes as I passed second.

"You're a goner bubble buns!"

I ran past third and heard the recess bell ring. I kept running. I lost it. My vision turned everything a shade of murky red as I pummeled toward the group of three skinny boys. In a flurry of punches, I hit each boy in the face again and again until they were on the ground. The rage kept me swinging; I didn't stop until I saw blood. The other children ran back inside the school, fleeing the scene. The three boys were left floundering helplessly behind the pitcher's mound in the corner of the playground. As I walked away, I spat at them.

"If I EVER hear it again you three will be eating your own teeth, got it?!"

No one ever used the word "bully" in the 1960's. There were no PTA meetings to discuss it, no training for teachers or parents to recognize or prevent it. Unfortunately, it just came with the territory of being a child in those days. This was the time of "boys will be boys," or "he's just teasing you because he likes you." There was no talk of compassion when it came to ten-year-olds. And God forbid you have something that makes you different as a child, because it also made you a target. My body taught me that I was different and that I was inferior to others around me.

Instead of being taught acceptance, I learned to fight.

I never told anyone about what happened on the playground that day. And to my appeasement, they shut their mouths from then on. My body became a battleground, something I needed to protect with violence against anyone who attacked it. Revenge felt good. Seeing the blood drip from their faces actually made me feel better. But, I also felt more alone than ever. I hid inside my body and it imprisoned me.

I'm fifty-six now and I still remember the way I felt when I was nine. Tears fill my eyes when I recall it, even now. I've done so much emotional work to recover and yet it still feels fresh, like an alcoholic recalling the time they tasted their first drop.

The next year I turned ten. When using the bathroom one day, I noticed a bright red splash of blood in my underwear and screamed. I thought my vagina had ripped open. I was crying when I ran outside to get my mother, who was busy entertaining a group of guests outside on our patio. I tugged on her skirt for attention.

"Mom," I whimpered, "there's blood in my underwear."

My mother calmly told me to go into her bathroom and get a maxi pad. I had no idea what was happening, and had never seen a pad or knew how to use one. On the way inside my sister intercepted me.

"If you got your period just use a tampon," she said as if I should have known. I felt stupid and ashamed.

In my mother's cabinet, I found a box labeled "Tampax," with a small paper pamphlet of instructions folded inside it. I stared wide-eyed at the side view of female anatomy, with a torpedo-like object going between the legs. I winced and struggled alone in the bathroom. With the tampon inside, I went back to the kitchen where my mother and sister were cleaning the guests' dishes. I cried huge salty tears as I turned to my mother. It hurt beyond belief. My sister asked if I put the tampon in and I affirmed, but it hurt so much I could barely move.

"Wait, Lu, you put it *where?*" my sister asked, sensing a mistake. With a few euphemisms and hand gestures, we uncovered the problem. I had inserted the tampon into my anus by mistake. My mother barely looked up from her dishes.

At thirteen, I was fewer than five feet tall and already over 135 pounds. I was depressed, moody, and hormonal. My mother never really mentioned the birds and the bees even after I got my period. Without guidance, I learned everything about sex from kids on the playground: a dramatic, scary, and inaccurate recount of where babies came from was exchanged through whispers. Sex education was never taught, never even mentioned. This only devastated me even further. It was one thing to be chubby, but to add to it my period—which I thought everyone could somehow "sense"—was unbearable.

At home, any mention of puberty was met with a hush. We were told "not to speak that way" on any matter pertaining to our growing bodies. My questions were swept under the rug to never be answered. Sex was seen as dirty—sinful even—and our bodies were an off-limits conversation.

By fourteen, my body continued to grow and take on a womanly form. I only wore a few outfits to school because I had outgrown almost everything. I tugged at shirts that showed my belly, pulled skirts down over my curvy thighs. Finally, after sensing my despair, my mother took me to a doctor to have an evaluation.

Surprisingly for the time, the doctor I visited was reasonable and fair. He delicately mentioned that my weight was too high for my age, and suggested I change the way I eat and explore more exercise. In reality, I was the enforcer of my new way of life, and unexpectedly, that gave me power. I have always been an extremely disciplined person, so I rose to the challenge. For the first time in my life, I actually evaluated what was being put into my body. I stopped drinking sodas and eating fried food altogether. I swapped scoops of ice cream for fruit and signed up for an aerobics class that happened three times a week at the neighborhood YMCA. Fortunately, I also grew a few inches in height, and that too helped balance the weight. Little by little, the pounds starting to fall away, and as they did, a happier and truer version of myself appeared—almost by *magic.*

Don't get me wrong, losing weight to feel good can be a dangerous game. I don't recommend going overboard! But I do believe harmony can be achieved when one is able to balance the way they eat, move, and are valued in the world as a woman. However, we must walk a fine line with caution. I still hear my inner voice sometimes when I catch my reflection in a mirror; I still hear the nagging, "five more pounds" when I see the number on the scale, or the chatter from people walking by saying, "such a pretty girl, only if she'd lose some weight!"

Sometimes I think I'll need to lose five pounds for the rest of my life no matter what weight I am. When we live in a society that values the way a woman looks rather than value her potential in the world, we subscribe to the ridiculous idea that thinner is always better. I know that's a harmful and dangerous thought. I'm not perfect, but I can catch my self-talk. I try to find compassion on the days I need it most. I try to quiet the echoing voices I still hear from those boys on the playground, but believe me, I still hear them.

Today, I am a mother of two boys only because I prayed to God that I wouldn't have any girls. (I guess he heard me!) The thought of reliving a childhood fraught with the pain of being heavy would simply be too much for me. When I was a child, every time my parents told me to pipe down when I had questions about my body it scarred me deeply. In an attempt to teach politeness and good Catholic values, they created more problems than they solved.

What they really were teaching me is that my questions didn't matter and that my opinions were better kept to myself.

Without support or guidance, I stumbled through the scary transition of becoming a woman.

I needed to hear the words, "I love you" a little more often. I needed to hear that sex was a beautiful thing that could happen between two people under the right circumstances. I needed to know that sex could be a pure and profound expression of love.

A painting hangs in my current home in West Palm Beach, Florida. It's the shape of a crescent moon on a woman's face. At the bottom, a quote reads,

"The entrance to someone's soul is a sacred honor."

This is what I continue to live, believe, and teach my children: the body is beautiful, and its entrance sacred. Love, sex, violence, and body image are all so intricately linked. We must tread lightly in a society that traps us unfairly into thinking we are only valuable in our appearance and sex appeal. We must continue to move through the world with respect and compassion for every shape, though it may be different from our own. We must continue to recognize that we are all unique emanations of God and deserve to be celebrated, not condemned, for our diversity.

Life Interrupted

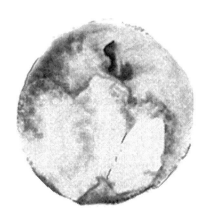

CHAPTER 3

NONCONSENSUAL INTERRUPTION

"I am willing to begin where I am right now to clean the rooms of my mental house." - Louise Hay

THE 1970'S WERE a time of radical change, both for me and for the world. I learned in my preteens something most people learn in their thirties: how to listen to my body, find balance, and properly nourish myself.

Life Interrupted

By the time I started middle school I was feeling more confident. My clothes no longer rubbed together at the seams, and I walked through life with my head a little higher than before.

Although, my feelings of rage, especially when it came to the opposite sex, simmered just below the surface the scars from my childhood had not left, even after the extra pounds had. I recalled the incident on the playground frequently, and the way it felt punching my classmates to the ground. I held close to the fact that if anyone tried to mess with me, I could take them. My newer, thinner body however got more positive attention than negative. In fact, they started coming out of the woodwork, which felt both good and scary at the same time.

In eighth grade, a boy named Eddie began passing notes to me in math class. We sat a couple rows apart, so any messages were vetted by the children that sat in between us. The first note I received I thought was for Cindy, the girl that sat behind me, so I passed it along without notice. Cindy opened the note and frowned.

She whispered, "This is for you Lu."

My heart sank. I peered through the classroom and saw Eddie looking at me. I unfolded the note to reveal a drawing of a strawberry milkshake, complete with Eddie and me drinking it on either side of a table facing each other. At the bottom was the standard grade school survey: three boxes, each awaiting a check mark that read, "yes," "no," and "maybe."

As any woman would, I checked the "maybe" box, giggled, and handed it back through the line. Eddie waited impatiently for the note's return. He opened it then shot me a confused and exhausted look which quickly morphed into a smile.

That afternoon, we walked side by side down the quaint suburban streets to Ferch's Malt Shoppe for strawberry shakes and to talk life. I could tell he was nervous. My stomach fluttered at the thought that a boy might like me, especially after the pain that stung my elementary school years. When he walked me back to my house I could tell he wanted to kiss me. He lingered awkwardly for a few minutes, strategizing his next move. As I began to say goodbye, he suddenly leaned towards me, lips puckered, eyes closed, determined. I was startled. Accidentally, he threw his whole body into me, exploding the strawberry shake I was holding between us. For a moment he paused, stunned, and looked back at me with wide eyes. Then as if nothing happened he politely said goodbye and ran in the opposite direction.

Needless to say, my first introductions to the opposite sex was somewhat awkward, but honestly, whose wasn't.

For sixth grade, I attended a Catholic private school which proved to be a stark change from the public elementary school that came before it. For one, the teachers were much stricter and often used public humiliation as means of discipline. My eighth-grade history teacher, Mr. Shula, was the harshest of them all.

To this day, I hate the subject of history. Mr. Shula's irresponsible tactics followed me through to adulthood. I subsequently struggled in every history course because of this fear. Mr. Shula would pose questions to the classroom then expect us to stand and give an answer. The standing was the cruel part—it made everyone in the room draw attention to your possible failure. When he called on me my body would shudder with the fear that I was his next victim.

Looking back, I can easily determine the source of Mr. Shula's anger. He was a gay man in the '70s unhappily teaching children at an uptight religious school. But at the time, I couldn't understand why he went to such lengths to embarrass us during the delicate time of adolescence.

Once, he called on me and asked a complicated question about The French Revolution. I stood to receive the torture. Even before he finished asking, I knew that I did not know the answer. I searched the classroom of faces staring. They looked back at me with panicked eyes.

"Didn't you read, Ms. Luann?" Mr. Shurla growled.

I had read. But what I read was so boring it went in one ear and out the other. My slow reading wasn't any help either. I fidgeted as I stood, looked at my shoes, and stuttered to find an answer.

He interrupted me, "What are you, STUPID?"

For the rest of class, I was forced to stand in the corner of the room with my face against the wall. I can still remember the way the tears tasted as the rolled down my cheeks and onto my lips.

I never wanted to be in school. Without much of an interest in any particular subject, I lacked motivation. Without many hobbies or sports, I never felt like there was anything particularly cool or interesting about me. I couldn't find a place where I fit, so instead, I looked elsewhere. As soon as I entered high school, I began working. Having a job made me feel productive and it gave me purpose. I didn't mind being in the adult world because I could relate to adults easily.

Though I didn't know it at the time, this was the very beginning of finding my gift.

But don't get me wrong, it took a while to find it! In fact, for years I believed I had nothing particularly valuable to offer to the world at all. But after many jobs, relationships, and rich experiences, I discovered that I possessed an insightful beyond my years: I was a deep thinker, and I possessed an "old soul"—like I had traversed parts of this life before.

Once I was able to tune into my inner voice, I found how to use my influence to help others.

Even small things, like working as a receptionist or cashier, allowed me to discover my passion to help others. Much later, I discovered this passion for helping others evolve into something even bigger: the ability to heal people from the wounds of life just as I healed my own.

It was the search for outside work that led to me hostessing at a local restaurant, which quickly led to cocktailing. Night after night, I would serve drinks and talk to older men that would overtly hit on me. Though it's strange to picture now, I was actually encouraged to drink on the job, and I would. A couple of sips of a white wine spritzer would help me relax and make me friendlier with customers. My ability to connect with adults sometimes worked too well, and men would linger a little too long in conversation, and I could feel their fingertips sometimes graze the small of my back as we talked.

As I progressed through high school, I ventured deeper into the murky unknown realm of men, bars, and underage drinking. Because I was a local, no one checked my ID, so I slipped into pretty much any bar unnoticed and often drank for free. It made me feel older and invincible. I started disassociating with my family, especially my parents who couldn't relate to my newfound freedom. Slowly their little girl was slipping into the strange world of adulthood.

It was during my nightly rounds that I stumbled into the Pipe Organ. I knew most of the staff there, so I snuck in, as usual, bypassing the bouncer at the door with a smile. I headed to an empty seat I found at the bar.

That was the first time I saw Dave. He was behind the bar, effortlessly moving from customer to customer, leaning inward to hear orders, mixing drinks with style and ease. I was captivated from the moment I laid eyes on him. He was tall, muscular, fluid in his movements and suave in his demeanor. It was busy that night, and it took a few minutes for him to notice me. I sat alone, crowded between two strangers. I leaned forward and set my elbows on the bar. Dave noticed me. His brown eyes pierced through the dimly lit bar.

He walked closer to me and smirked as he spoke, "And what are you having, little lady?"

The attraction was instantaneous. Something sparked between us that night—a gentle flame that grew into romance. He was older than me, in his late twenties, and I was only seventeen. Though it wasn't a terribly big age difference, it was amplified by the fact that I was still at high school, whereas he was an adult man in the working world. He was forbidden and intoxicating. I was drawn to him immediately.

Soon after, we began to date. I would wait for him to finish work at the bar, sometimes until the early hours of the morning, and then we would sip drinks and talk at his apartment. At first, it felt like I was in an adult relationship. It made me feel empowered to date someone like Dave. I couldn't relate to any of the boys in my class, as they all seemed too immature. Dave filled me with confidence and desire.

As our relationship continued, my family began to express their disapproval. My brothers were protective and didn't like the idea that I was spending time with an older man. My parents were especially wary of the fact that he was way older than me and that he was a bartender. They hated that I was away from the house more than ever.

At the time, I was too naive to notice the warning signs that were undeniable to my family. But over time, a fluttering feeling would happen in my stomach at certain points in our relationship. I know now that my instincts were screaming at me to get away from this man. But being young, inexperienced, and blinded by romance proved to be a dangerous combination.

Dave had a tendency to drink. I rationalized that this was par for the course being a bartender. And if anything, I thought it made him interesting. But then on several occasions when we were out together, I noticed that Dave had gone overboard. His drinking was fun to a point, but too much booze made him violent, angry, and stupid.

One night he came to pick me up. I watched from the upstairs window as he pulled his cougar into the driveway. Usually, he would get out to greet me, but this time he obnoxiously laid on the horn and yelled my name into the dusky evening.

"Let's go, Lu!" He yelled.

My younger brother John noticed this before I did and seethed with aggression. He stormed out the front door to confront him. I watched them shouting at each other from my bedroom and froze with fear. Then, things escalated. My heart sank in disbelief as my brother flung the driver's door open, pulled Dave out as if he was plucking a blade of grass from the earth. Dave started swinging completely out of control towards my brother, who retaliated like a madman. I screamed as I pushed between them. Once separated, they spat and panted like wild dogs.

John implored me not get in the car that night, but I brushed him off. As far as I was concerned my family was just getting in the way of me living my life. Their pleas to stay away from Dave fell on deaf ears.

I slammed the passenger door and yelled at Dave to drive. He screeched the car backward, leaving dark tire marks on our driveway. As he shifted the car forward he turned to look at me. His hair was greasy and tousled. His skin was damp with sweat. His eyes were unfocused, and when he spoke I could smell the brandy on his breath.

"I'll kill your brother if that happens again."

The sour feeling in my stomach rose upward to my throat. Though my young adolescent brain hadn't made the connection that Dave was dangerous, my female intuition had. It had been trying to warn me all along.

While I knew Dave tended to drink too much and get violent, I never thought that violence would turn on me. I thought his quick temper was just part of his personality. It even made him sexy at times. As things became more serious in the relationship, Dave became increasingly possessive. Sometimes, he would show up at my house unannounced and demanded I leave with him. He was jealous when I even spoke to another man. Sometimes, he teased me too much and got carried away with insults.

On New Year's Eve, we went to a hotel where my sis and her husband were, so we could stay the night. They gave us a room to stay in and we planned on going to a party together with them at the Marriott. It was the first time I been in a hotel with a boyfriend, and I felt sophisticated. We checked in together, giggling like newlyweds. As the sun went down and the day turned to night, we opened a bottle of brandy and started drinking. I never liked brandy much but I wanted to celebrate, so I poured myself a glass.

A few hours later, I started feeling chills, like I was coming down with a bad cold. I stopped after one glass of booze, but Dave, well I stopped counting after six! All I wanted to do was go to bed and call it a night. I felt sick. Dave was getting sloppy. He was falling all over me, kissing and laughing. His breath was thick with liquor; his hands were reaching up my skirt. I walked towards the hotel bed and told him I wasn't feeling well. I wanted to get some sleep. But, unfortunately, that's not what he had in mind. He abruptly walked around to my side of the bed.

"I want SEX! I didn't come all this way for nothing!" He screamed. The sheer volume of his voice frightened me. He was barely able to stand, swaying stupidly beside the hotel bed.

I yelled back at him and told him I wasn't feeling well, and that he should just leave me alone. That's when he got angry. Before I could even understand what happened, Dave swung his arms madly and slapped me hard on the face. I was utterly shocked.

"You can take me home now," I muttered.

I felt anger pulsing through his body.

He mocked me: "Ok, *princess!* I will take you home to *Mommy and Daddy.*"

I was scared. It was like someone else was speaking through his body. I didn't recognize this strange demon, but I knew for certain I needed to get out.

Through terrifying silence, Dave found his keys and headed towards the door. I should have called a cab. No one in their right mind would drive with him in this state, but I had no choice. And since he was taking me home, I was relieved. I didn't want to say anything else that might antagonize him, so I buckled my seatbelt and literally said a prayer. He drove recklessly through the abandoned streets just a few moments before midnight. I feared for my life.

About a month later, Dave knew my parents were out of town for the weekend. I had mentioned it him, thinking it might be a cool place for us to hang out. After all, we were always at his place and I wasn't old enough to have my own apartment yet. The best I could do was host when my whole family was gone, which sounded mature. I lit some candles and dressed up for him. I had no idea I was in any kind of danger.

When he opened the door, I immediately knew he was drunk. He kissed me forcibly and invited himself inside. As usual, he helped himself to my parent's alcohol cabinet. I watched anxiously as one drink turned to two, then three, then four. He was sucking down brandy fast with his feet carelessly propped on my parent's nice furniture. I worried he might break something in his state, but I didn't know what to do.

After he slugged his fifth glass, he looked at me and asked, "Where's your bedroom?"

We had never even been there before. I refused to tell him. I knew something terrible was about to happen. Before

I could escape, he forced me into the nearest bedroom—our guest room—and started making out with me.

I had been a virgin after all.

I wanted romance and love—all the things most girls want—but instead, my boyfriend was raping me.

***

I had to end it with Dave, but I didn't know how. Looking back I wish I had talked to someone—anyone!—about what had happened.

Instead I chose secrecy and isolation. It proved to be the wrong decision, and I know this now.

If you, reader, can relate to any of this please take action accordingly. No one deserves to go through what I went through. No one has to suffer alone.

When I broke it off with Dave on the phone, he was livid. He begged me to reconsider, but I knew what I had to do. He called my house all hours of the night, drunk, rambling, and upset, screaming for me to take him back, but I refused.

Then, one night he showed up at my house unannounced. In a drunken rage, he pounded on my front door. My parents called the police immediately. At this point, he was breaking the law. Over the next few months, the cops came three more times. My father was fed up. I remember the night I signed the paperwork at the police station, eventually resorting to a restraining order. A heavy sigh exited my lungs. Only if everyone had known the restraining order was too little too late.

With Dave a safe distance away, the last few months of my adolescence calmed down. No more police cars in my parent's driveway, no more late night phone calls, no more fits of rage and pressures to have sex. I continued to work as a waitress and was happy making money outside of school.

Still, I had a recurring idea that it was time to get out of Milwaukee. After graduation, I felt like the time had come and passed for me to be living in the same town where I was raised. I became increasingly restless, looking for the next move, the next job, and maybe the next boyfriend. I wasn't sure where I wanted to go, but I was open to the possibility of exploring a new city.

Then, one night, after I had finished my cocktailing shift, I walked to my car alone through the dark streets. The night was still and quiet and the lights from the bar faded behind me. The streetlights overhead were the only source of light, and between each one, my stomach sank. Something felt off.

Then, I heard a voice say, "Hey sweet thing..."

The voice sounded familiar, but I wasn't sure. As I turned my head in its direction, I saw no one. For a moment I thought it was just the cooks from the kitchen trying to scare me, as we often pranked each other. My pace quickened towards my blue two-door Buick. My intuition spoke up again. "Be careful!"

My hands shook furiously as I tried to unlock the vehicle. I knew someone was close—I could feel it. Out of the darkness, a man leaped toward me and pinned my shoulders up against the driver's side window. He slammed his hand into my chest, and for a second it took my breath away. I struggled, flailing my arms and legs as hard as I could. I tried to look at his face but it was too dark.

From the depths of my stomach, I opened my mouth to scream. I pushed from my lungs but nothing came out. I struggled for anything, a noise, a word, something for someone to come help me. Under the streetlamps of a cold October night, the only noise was the clumsy exchange of arms and legs as I resisted him. *Only silence came from my mouth.*

Then, as quickly as he appeared he was gone. He bolted back into the night. Maybe he saw someone walking in his direction, but I didn't care to find out. I needed safety fast. Shaking and crying, I opened the car door, but just as I ignited the engine he reemerged, grabbed the door handle and tried to get in the car. I slammed on the gas, swerving like crazy.

That night I decided it was time for me to leave Milwaukee.

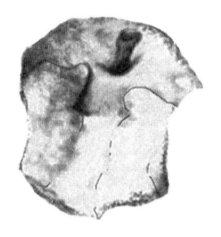

CHAPTER 4

THE INTERRUPTED SHIFT

"To release the past we must be willing to forgive."
— Louise Hay

THERE WAS NO better time for me to meet Susan. She was a supervisor at American Airlines and would frequent The Packing House Restaurant, where I worked, a few nights a week with some of her coworkers. They would come in looking exhausted and sit in a booth near the back, recounting their endless shifts over bottles of wine. Susan always had a way to make everyone laugh, and she was a blast to be around.

One night, deep in the winter months, a blizzard was blowing through town and Susan happened to be at the bar. Because she lived closer than I did to the airport, she invited me to stay the night at her place, drink a bottle of wine and wait for the storm to pass. I agreed. We drove through the blustery storm back to her apartment. Susan popped the cork on a bottle of Cabernet and handed me a glass as I sat on her couch. We got to talking about Milwaukee life, our frustrations, and where we saw our young lives headed in the future. We both agreed that we didn't want to stay.

What started as a drunken joke felt more and more serious as the night went on.

We both knew there had to be more to life than what we were living, and in our youthful naïveté, we were eager to chase it.

On a whim, we started throwing out ideas.

"Florida?" Susan mused.

"No," I responded. I hated Disney.

"California?"

"No way!" I exclaimed. "Earthquakes!"

We were quiet for a moment. The whole world was open to us to explore. We could go anywhere and the possibilities seemed endless.

"What about Arizona?" Susan said, "My father lives in Scottsdale."

I had no objections to Arizona, and I thought it was helpful that Susan already had family there. I imagined it sunny, open, and free. I could see myself there, starting a new job and a new life. We clinked our glasses to celebrate our decision. I knew there had to be more out there than just Milwaukee, Wisconsin.

Because Susan worked for the airport, we had an opportunity to fly just about anywhere. Later that week, she called me and asked if I had the afternoon free, and I did. She suggested that we drive to Chicago, hop on a flight to Arizona, see if we liked it, then take the redeye back to Milwaukee. I was overjoyed at an adventure and to see the potential Arizona had to offer.

"But there's one thing," Susan interrupted, just as I was getting excited. "When we get to the airport, you have to pretend you're a flight attendant, and that you work for me.

The security guard will ask you for your pass, and you have to pretend that you forgot it in your car. That way, we can sneak onboard and fly for free."

I agreed and giggled nervously. A grand adventure awaited us.

When we arrived in Chicago, we approached the security guard at the counter, who was (luckily!) a man. Susan went ahead of me, flashed her pass, and started to walk towards the gate. When it was my turn, I mustered up all the acting I could and rummaged through my bag with increasing stressfulness. The ticket agent looked at me over his glasses.

"Oh no, Sue, I think I forgot my pass!" I exclaimed as I dug even more frantically through my purse. She played along.

"What do you mean? Are you sure? Is it in the car?"

The guard leaned over the counter.

"That's OK, sweetheart, hurry back to your vehicle and grab the pass; I'll hold the flight until you return."

"But you don't understand, sir, my car is in Milwaukee! And this is a mandatory flight attendant meeting in Phoenix! Oh no, what am I going to do?"

He bought it and let us through.

Susan turned to me.

"You in?" she asked. And I was.

While flying into Phoenix we opened a bottle of wine. We taxied our way to a beautiful restaurant on one of the highest peaks in El Tapatio.

When I returned to Milwaukee, I broke the news to my parents that I was moving. Surprisingly, they were supportive. They wished me nothing but the best. I already knew that even if they disapproved, I still would have left. I had a mind of my own and knew there was more to see in this world! And so I packed my bags, said my goodbyes, and left.

We found a two-bedroom apartment in Scottsdale. Though I had no jobs lined up, I was filled with optimism. I left it up to chance, faithful that fate would unfold in my favor.

One morning, shortly after I moved, something very unusual happened to me. While I was getting dressed, I caught a glimpse of myself in the bathroom mirror. While my mind could process the image—the blue pajamas, the messy brown hair, the olive skin—

I realized at the same time I didn't know who I was looking at. It was a strange feeling that I had never experienced before. I felt like an outsider, a stranger, an unfamiliar face, as if I was having an out-of-body experience.

While there had been dozens of times I saw my reflection and felt insecure, like I needed to lose weight or I was getting old, but this wasn't that. This was much deeper.

I saw my own reflection and fundamentally did not know who I was. I gazed endlessly into my own eyes for recognition but I only found someone confused and lost. I didn't know who I was anymore.

Though shaken, I shut the light off in the bathroom and walked out. I wanted to keep moving forward in my life. I wanted to find a job and home where I belonged so I could feel happy in my own skin. I hated this feeling of the unknown and I was ready to find myself.

When I was around eight years old, we used to vacation in the Cayman Islands when you could catch oysters right off the shore. On Seven Mile Beach, a man would sell them for five dollars apiece. It was a small price, and well worth the gamble to see what kind of pearl was waiting inside.

I chose one to try my luck. I peered into the bucket, through the murky water, and saw the grey, rough and shapeless shells, sealed shut with no indications of their treasures inside. I would choose the one that spoke to me, the one my heart wanted, and watch the man pull the dripping shell from the bucket to reveal my fate. I wondered, what is waiting in the oyster that I have chosen?

The truth is that you can never know for certain what life has in store for you. And many only pursue life for the biggest and most valuable pearl waiting inside. But things are not always as they seem. If you have the courage to look deeper, you'll find that the rarest and most unique pearls are imperfect, in every shape, size, and color. What's truly valuable is the strength to see deeper, and hold close to the faith that God is giving you exactly what you need in every moment that you allow.

I see life as this game of choosing oysters, both then as a child, and now as an adult. It has only been through celebrating my uniqueness that I was ever able to harness my self-worth.

In Arizona, I continued to search for myself in every new opportunity that came my way. I searched the newspaper ads and called each one that looked remotely interesting. I knew a fantastic pearl could possibly be hiding inside an unassuming shell. In a short amount of time, I was a waitress, a cashier, and a magazine salesperson. Sometimes the paths led me to dead ends,

but I refused to feel negative about any passing experience: every new job gave me an opportunity to look inside myself and discover more about my true self.

In June, while I was selling magazine subscriptions, I saw a newspaper ad for the Miss Scottsdale Beauty pageant. It was 1982. The ad took up the entire back page of the Scottsdale Times. The words, "Could you be the next Miss Scottsdale?" were sprawled in huge yellow letters. A photo below showed the most beautiful women I had ever seen, each in a different glittering gown, standing proudly on a stage with hundreds of spectators. I peered deeply into the pixelated faces of each of these women. I searched them for meaning, for beauty, for identity. They looked talented, fearless and proud. They looked like winners. Without hesitation, I ripped the ad and stuffed it into my pocket unnoticed by anyone.

Once home from work, I pulled out the crumpled ad and smoothed it on my kitchen counter. An audition would take place in ten days, at two pm, at the Scottsdale Recreation Center, just a few blocks from where Susan and I lived. There would be an interview to begin, then a swimsuit contest and formal gown portion to find the next Miss Scottsdale. I was intrigued. The thought of being in a swimsuit on stage was unnerving, to say the least. I looked again at those women's faces in the photo. I wanted to feel empowered and confident like them, swimsuit or not. Right away I called the number in the ad to reserve my spot for the audition. I told no one.

On the day of the competition, I stuffed a periwinkle colored swimsuit and black silky gown into my purse and left work early. I told my boss I wasn't feeling well. I drove to the Rec Center, where a line of anxious women gathered in the baking sun. Interviews were held in a gold-colored conference room where a panel of mostly men sat with uninterested faces. When my turn came, I sat in a plastic folding chair and faced my fate.

They started with my name, birthplace, and my age. I started to relax. Charisma came easily to me. I cracked jokes to ease the tension. I smiled and tossed my brown curls that were sprayed crisp with hairspray. This was going to be a breeze. Then the judge sitting at the end, a sallow-looking man with a balding head and wrinkled khaki overcoat delivered his final request, "Luann can you please walk for us?"

For a second I froze. I thought of the empty girl in the mirror. Her eyes flashed in my mind—the confused, lost look of someone I couldn't recognize. I searched her face, her clothes, and her hair for beauty. I opened my mouth to answer but no response came out. Who was she? *Was she beautiful?* I couldn't shake the persistence of the question, its uncertainty pounding on me like a hail storm. I rose from my seat and walked in front of the judges.

They whispered among themselves and then the man leaned toward the microphone.

"Congratulations, Luann. You have qualified for the final round."

I felt extraordinarily happy to be in the final round. But when I remembered the swimsuit crumpled in the bottom of my purse, a pang of insecurity tightened my stomach. I took a deep breath and told myself to muster all the confidence I could. I slipped into the bathroom among a zoo of other girls, some happy and others devastated. Emotions circulated in the stuffy room. I scrambled to get into my swimsuit. As I opened the safety pin I was given to secure my audition number, a wave of nausea washed over me. Was I just a number in a swimsuit? Did I not deserve even a name as I paraded my body in front of a group of men to judge it?

I decided I should at least give it a shot, and anyway, it was just about time to line up. I took one last look at myself through the flurry of women putting on their finishing touches. There I stood: heavy makeup, curled stiff hair, bright high-cut swimsuit, and six-inch silver heels. It was almost laughable. I still didn't recognize myself, but instead of frightening it felt humorous. Like a little girl trying on all of mommy's dress up clothes.

As number thirty-nine, I lined up behind forty and ahead of thirty-eight. The line was already moving to head on stage. I mustered my best model walk and strutted through the stage door. The blasting lights blinded my eyes, but I kept walking. When my number was called I walked downstage and did my best to look natural. On the inside, I was burning, filling with regret and trembling with anger. I could make out the same judges who had interviewed me sitting in the front row of the audience. While they seemed ordinary in the interview, now they seemed completely repugnant. I hated them; I hated their judging eyes and disgusting stares. They didn't deserve to see my body, and I was more than just flesh. Anger overtook me.

I walked back to the line of contestants. I realized my confidence was soaring when I entered this pageant, and now it felt so low I could barely stand it. I thought about the way I felt when I saw first saw the beauty pageant ad. Forty-nine other women stood beside me, each gorgeous in their own right, but now they just looked sad and very alone. I didn't feel beautiful or confident at all.

The emcee was about to announce the winner, and the lights dimmed on stage. Instead of terror or anticipation, I simply wanted to leave. I peered through the wings and found the exit. I walked out the doors of the recreation center and on to the cool, dry street. It was dusk and the beautiful desert sky was blushing a soft pink and orange. Instantly I felt relief. My heels clicked on the pavement as I found my car, and slipped inside to escape. I promised myself that I would never let anyone make me feel the way the judges had on that day. I didn't need anyone or anything to confirm that my real beauty couldn't be judged by the eyes. My real worth was deep inside, waiting for the right opportunity to manifest.

After a while, I quit selling magazines. It had been a fun job and a nice company to work for, but door to door sales was tough, and I had little success making commissions. I jumped from job to job, continuing to try on different positions to find my voice. I felt connected to an inner strength that encouraged me to keep looking, keep trying.

The unfolding of new experiences set me into rapid motion. I was constantly in a state of reinvention.

Ready for a new change, I applied for a job at the "Park and Fly" shuttle service to Phoenix airport. It was there I first met Gino. I had an instant attraction to him and felt romance right off the bat. After a brief interview, he hired me on the spot. Though I prayed that he was single, I soon found out that he was married, but it didn't stop our flirtatious dance.

One night, Gino asked me to meet him and some other co-workers for a drink, so I did. "Total Eclipse of the Heart" was playing in the bar that night—a foreshadowing of what was to happen between Gino and me. I look back on that evening and see where it all started. That night, we were inseparable. We created a whole universe between us, one where no one else existed. We laughed and drank and danced. It was all new and exhilarating.

For the next few months, we snuck around, talked a lot, kissed a lot, and, eventually, made love—but only once. With Gino, it wasn't about the sex, he was never aggressive like my previous lovers had been. Instead, he was emotional. He made me feel so special and loved. He vaguely reminded me of my father: sweet, charming, Italian and loving.

It was easy to see that we were both falling in love. Whenever I mentioned his wife, he simply said he had "gotten married for the wrong reasons." They had met young—in their teens—and her parents tragically died in a car accident. He pitied her and didn't have the heart for her to be alone, so they married. He looked sad anytime he mentioned her, often saying he "loved her but was never in love with her." That sentiment made me see a glimmer of hope for us to be together. Maybe, I was the one he was truly in love with, and maybe someday that would manifest into lasting love.

However, things at work became tense. I was promoted to manager, and controlling a group of men proved to be difficult. Once the news of Gino, and I was out, I was treated even worse by the staff. Though no one outwardly mentioned our affair, I could tell in the little snickers that would come from Gino's brothers and friends. The constant judgments made me wonder if the job was worth it.

Then one lazy Sunday afternoon, I was perusing the shops in downtown Scottsdale to add to the latest reinvention of my wardrobe. It was August—a hot and sticky afternoon. I saw a quaint store situated on the corner of Fifth Avenue and Scottsdale Road. Overhead a black elegant awning read the words "Alexia Natural Fashions." Curious, I stepped inside, a relief from the extremely dry, late-summer heat. Still new to the Southwest, I hadn't yet adjusted to the desert.

The first thing my hands touched in the boutique was raw silk, something I had never felt before. I walked into the store and was compelled towards it with all of my senses. I picked up a raw silk scarf in powder blue. Instantly, the Arizona heat subsided from my body. The texture was like a cloud, creamy and delicate.

The saleswoman noticed me and remarked, "Isn't it heaven?"

I answered her question with my own: "Are you hiring?"

Life Interrupted

In less than a week, I was walking back down Fifth Avenue for my first official shift at Alexia's. My suede heels clicked along the cement pavement while the August heat engulfed me. I had left Gino and the Park and Fly the second I knew I could be happier elsewhere. Though I cared for him deeply, our love had run cold. I couldn't wait forever for things to change in his marriage, and I felt guilty to keep sneaking around the issue. So once I was hired at Alexia's, I quit and didn't look back. I didn't even have any fashion or retail experience, but still, I was made for the job. I loved the beauty of the boutique, the raw silk, and the dripping chandelier earrings. It felt like a place I wanted to stay and play.

When you lead with your heart, the natural abundance of life will flow.

It only took a few weeks before I realized I had a true gift for sales. I was out-earning some associates that had been working there for years. My heart filled with passion when it came to the boutique. Because my calling was unfolding in front of me, every day felt exciting. Even the tedious and mundane aspects of the job felt fun. I loved the feeling of stocking the raw silk dresses that hung elegantly arranged by color. I loved cleaning the jewelry cases and making the store shine. I loved surrounding myself with women because they made me feel safe.

By January, about six months in, I was setting records for the highest sales in history. I made generous commissions and starting feeling financially stable for the first time in my life. What drove me was the rush I would get from making other women feel good about themselves. I cherished the times when women would transform in front of my eyes. They would come in feeling fearful, insecure, hating this or that about their figures, and I met them with hope. I had tons of ideas about how to make it better, and I could tell from their eyes they were tired of looking.

I would situate my customers in front of a floor-to-ceiling mirror that was divided in three. I would gaze deep into their reflections and often find a woman that was tired, sad, or fearful. I would see an anxious soul that really needed to feel good about themselves. With my creativity and patience, I painted the blank canvases. With every new outfit and matching shoes, I felt like I had made a small but significant change. My heart grew with gratitude; I was giving the feeling I had so long wished to receive.

Life Interrupted

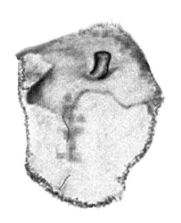

CHAPTER 5

REFUSING MEDIOCRITY

"I can never stand still. I must explore and experiment."
– Walt Disney

MY FLAIR FOR sales at Alexia's landed me a full-time management position in beautiful Laguna Beach, California. I was excited to leap into a new place of opportunity. Within two weeks of receiving the offer, I packed up my belongings and said my goodbyes to Susan.

Life Interrupted

Our separation seemed natural at this point—we are already started to drift apart, and I welcomed a reason to go in a new direction.

Also, I called Gino one last time. Though we hadn't spoken in months, I thought the least I could do was say goodbye before I left. When I told him, he didn't believe me. He thought I was just kidding, but I was anything but. I explained to him that I loved him, but couldn't wait any longer for him. I needed to move on with my life and I had received an excellent career move I couldn't refuse in California. He was so shocked I could almost hear his jaw hit the floor. I hung up, sighed, and moved on, onto bigger things.

Back in Arizona, a friend had given me a contact for an apartment. I had the address scribbled on a scrap of paper, and after much searching, I found the beautiful craftsman home just a mile from Alexia's. When I knocked on the door, a woman whipped open the door.

"Are you here for the room?"

I said that I was and her face suddenly turned sad.

"I'm so sorry, but the room is no longer available."

I went back to my car and cried. What was I supposed to do? I knew not one soul in California and nowhere to go. I drove around a bit and eventually found a diner. There, I called my sister back in Wisconsin. Hopefully, she would have a business contact that would rescue me.

"No problem, Lu!" she answered.

Instantly I felt relief. Turns out, a client of hers had an eighty-five-foot yacht on Balboa Island and said I could stay as long as I want, for free! The only catch was I had to be out on the weekends, as he rented it for events.

I stayed in the yacht for the first few months in California—living in a dream. I would wake up to chirping seagulls and breezy coastal air. At night I was lulled to sleep by the calm waves. After a few months, however, I quickly learned that free is never really free, and I anxiously looked elsewhere for a new home.

It was through a newspaper ad that I found Ruth, an older woman who had a room for rent in Mission Viejo. She took me under her wing as if I was her own daughter. Our birthdays were a day apart, so maybe that explained why we got along so well. I stayed with Ruth for about a year until I got a new job at Brustles Couture on Fashion Island in

Newport Beach. Then I met Leslie and her daughter, and I stayed with them in another room on Balboa Island.

Needless to say, I jumped around a bit. While my home life was somewhat unpredictable, my career was thriving. I found myself evolving into the role of manager. I began to understand the clientele I was serving and I took my role of service in their lives seriously. I especially loved when women came into the store for a specific reason, like a job interview, travel, or a special date. I had a knack for turning their doubts into confidence, and that's where I thrived. My passion was triple-fold, I loved being in charge, I loved helping women, and (of course) I loved making the commission on the sales.

In true California fashion, I decided to try an acting course to see if I was any good. I always had a flair for theater, and I thought with a little coaching I might discover some hidden talent. Even my penchant for sales was rooted in my innate ability to pretend. I asked a friend of mine, Leslie, who was already a working actress where I might be able to find an instructor. She was somewhat successful and seemed to love the craft.

"Julian Smith," she said without hesitation, "He'll make or break you."

It was still the 80's, and so when I got back to my apartment, I pulled out the yellow pages and flipped to the directory. I found the listing for Julian's class, *The Actor's Den*, and I called the number. There was still a few spots open in his upcoming workshop, so I booked it right away. Forty-nine dollars got me six weeks of acting lessons, and who knows what could come of it?

Leslie was right about Julian. And, after a few weeks in his class, I started to believe he was more in the business of "breaking" people rather than "making" them. He was harsh, but passionate. His classes were intense, and sometimes they brought back memories of my painful childhood. Nevertheless, I was determined. I hoped my reborn California-self could tackle any criticism, and it helped that I was pretty damn good at acting. Even Julian thought so, which made him especially tough on me.

The first thing Julian emphasized was that in order to be an artist you had to be vulnerable. He had ways of digging into your deepest insecurities, exposing them on stage, and making you a more honest performer because of it. It was both transformational and a little crazy. Sometimes he took the power dynamic a little too far.

Once, Julian had each one of us stand and face the class while they yelled out judgments based only on our appearances. This was a way of finding how people see you as an actor, and how you read physically.

When I stood, the feedback was mostly positive. "Pretty!" I heard someone say. "Girl next door." "Humble." "Demure." "Soft." Others were not as complimentary. "Sneaky," someone said, and I was surprised. "Distrustful." "Snooty." "Mean." Talk about being vulnerable!

Our next assignment was to tell a story to the class and make them laugh and then cry. I instantly knew the story of my first tampon experience would surely bust everyone up. I was right. I took the stage, a one-woman show, and relived the experience. All at once I was ten years old again, becoming a woman all too soon. When I delivered the final punch my whole class laughed. I laughed too, and it felt good to finally feel relief on that topic. Even as a young adult the pain was still tender in my heart, and using my pain to make others laugh was deeply therapeutic.

Though I didn't know it, I was beginning to find therapy in expressing myself. Although much of Julian's techniques were questionable, he knew what he was doing. He was unearthing parts of us that we kept buried and hidden, and using them to make us better.

Once the laughter about the tampon story dissipated, I approached my next task of making everyone cry—not an easy request at all. Julian decided to paint a picture of my mother on her deathbed. I kneeled on the ground and began to speak to her. I pretended to take my mother's hand and cradle it to my chest. I spoke my final words before she ascended into heaven.

After a few minutes of this, it became too real. I thought of my mother with her loving eyes and warm heart. I considered the heavy fact that she *would* be on her way out one day. Tears welled up in my eyes. I began to think about my relationship to her, my entire life, being her daughter— the mistakes and untold things I wish I could have said. I looked up and the whole class was crying too. Wow, maybe I was onto something with this acting thing!

Unfortunately, Julian was getting to me. For as much as he pushed me to new heights creatively, it came at a cost. He was aggressive and insulting sometimes. His passion was both helpful and harmful to his students. Some couldn't take it and dropped out early, but I remained on the fence. I knew he saw potential in me and I liked that. I kept coming to class in spite of some of the hesitations I felt in my gut.

Julian's next assignment was similar to his last. He was all about making you feel and making the audience feel with you. Instead of sadness, this time the emotion was fear. We each had to select from a few classic horror scenes and reenact them. I chose Hitchcock, naturally, thinking I could do a pretty good Marion Crane.

When it was time to show our pieces I felt confident. I had studied my subject and took notes on her nuances. It was exciting to feel the whole class watching me in suspense. I began to charade taking a shower, washing my hair, looking feminine and vintage. My classmate pulled back the invisible curtain and stabbed at me. Just like the last, this assignment came true to life fast.

I found myself pretending to be afraid and then actually being afraid.

Instantly, the night with the attacker came back to me. I remembered hearing the footsteps as I was walking to my car, the eerie, terrible, sickening feeling that someone was coming after me. Meanwhile, my classmate diligently continued to act out his part. His brow furrowed as he looked me straight in the eyes and attacked. It was too real, all of it.

"I opened my mouth to scream, partly for the assignment and partly for real".

I took a moment to realize that I wasn't actually screaming, and it brought me back into the room. My eyes met Julian's and I remembered that this was only pretend. He looked disappointed. He crossed his arms and opened one palm up to the ceiling as if to say, "Where's the scream?"

I asked if we could start over and Julian agreed, but he didn't look happy. My heartbeat pounded in my chest with adrenaline. I was scared, vulnerable, and also bewildered. We went through the scene again— all the details I had studied so closely, but it was hard to focus. As my classmate pulled back the curtain a second time, I pushed so hard with my lungs but no noise came out at all. I was consumed with a feeling of helplessness. It felt like a nightmare I had experienced many times before.

My classmate and I tried the scene again and failed. The same thing happened. For some reason or another, I just couldn't scream. Julian was losing his temper.

"Come on, Lu, what's the problem? This man is about to kill you. Where's the fear?"

"I'm trying," my voice was weak, "I can't seem to scream."

Julian looked at me like that was a stupid thing to say.

"This is theater." He began and I already knew where it was going. "Exposing yourself emotionally is the only way your audience will believe you. I need you to go there. I need you to commit."

The thought of trying to scream again and feel that awful sense of hopelessness was too much. It was too painful and real to be reminded of the events of that terrible night, especially when I wouldn't get out of the scene alive. I was terrified, exhausted and confused. I told Julian I didn't want to do the scene again and he shouldn't push me.

"This is MY classroom" he snarled. "My rules. You have a career Luann, you know that. You might be my top student in this group. Why are you sabotaging yourself? If you want the part, scream, Lu. Scream now and show me fear."

"No," I said, and I walked out.

I had found my limit. Julian was harassing me and it needed to stop. I didn't care what kind of an actress I could have been; I'd rather just be myself.

With the acting class gone, I focused on managing Brustles. I didn't realize what a weight I had been carrying until I let it go. Instead, I filled my days with fashion, happiness, and friendship.

One afternoon after a busy day at the boutique, my dear friend Barb came to visit. We were chatting on the couch deciding where to go for lunch when the phone rang. The energy was so intense I physically jumped at the noise. I went to the kitchen, picked up the receiver, and before I even said hello a voice said, "Lu? Is that you?

I knew immediately it was Gino. I recognized his voice even when he had only muttered a syllable. I felt my heart plunge into my chest and tighten every muscle in my body. My hands began to shake and my voice was soft.

"Gino?"

"Lu," his voice was hushed and relieved. "Please listen for a second."

Barb came into the kitchen after a few minutes. She could tell I was shaken by the call and looked concerned. She asked me several times who was on the line, but I couldn't answer her. I was listening intently to Gino, searching for any insight into his intentions.

Barb found a scrap of paper and a pen in my kitchen. She scribbled a silent message and slid the paper to me across the kitchen counter. It read, "Are you OK?"

I nodded. I told Gino I would see him and quickly ended the call. As soon as I plunged the phone back onto the kitchen wall, Barb spoke up.

"Luann, who in the world was that!? You're shaking! Are you OK?"

I didn't know how to answer her. It was true that Gino had gotten to me. Just the sound of his voice took me back to our time together, and it made me anxious. What on Earth did he have to say to me? What was there left to say at all?

I tried to explain the story to Barb, but she just looked back at me with confusion. There was really no easy way to explain what had happened. I felt shameful again and didn't want Barb's judgment. My previous life in Phoenix had been a distant memory.

"Listen, I don't know who that is or why he called," Barb said. "But, what I do know is, he affected you, and not in a good way."

It was hard to ignore that she was right. Sometimes female friends have an intuition when it comes to what's right for their friends. I felt that in this moment. I felt her concern for me and maybe the fact that Gino was a bad choice altogether.

Despite knowing this, I still went to meet him. I wanted to hear what he had to say. He had somehow tracked me down in California; I figured at least I could listen to what he had to say.

The next evening, I agreed to meet Gino down by the water at the Laguna Beach Inn. It was a lovely hotel that sat right on the water's edge—a picturesque view of California life. Still, I wasn't sure what type of conversation I would be having with him, and if I even wanted it. The anxiety overtook me. I could feel my heart pounding in my chest as I walked to the hotel's entrance. The hostess led me out to the patio. It was a beautiful day, and the expansive Pacific Ocean glittered for miles in every direction.

Then I saw him. Gino was sitting at a corner table, his eyes darting around in anticipation. He was wearing a blue collared shirt with stripes, black pants, and a shiny belt. His hair was combed straight back and it glinted in the sun. As soon as he saw me he stood up. I walked towards him, unsure as to how we should greet. Before I could decide he threw his arms around me and squeezed my small frame up against his. I suddenly had a feeling how this conversation was going to unfold.

Over the course of the evening, Gino spilled his heart to me. The sun gradually fell behind the horizon and the evening dusk was casting long shadows on the beach walkers that drifted in the distance. I sipped my mojito as I looked into Gino's eyes. He still looked good— unfortunately—and in some ways, I longed to just fall back into the ease that I felt when we were together. There was no doubt we had a connection. I felt that in his presence, his jokes, and his touch. Maybe in some other life, Gino and I could have made each other happy.

When the stars began to emerge in the sky, Gino told me officially what he had come to say all along: That he had left his wife Jackie and that he wanted to be with me. It was everything I had wanted to hear only much too late. As I looked into his dark brown eyes I knew that there was no way we were going to be together. After all, if he had left his wife and children, who knew what he would do to me? I didn't want to take that chance. I was a new woman, with a new job, successful and living in beautiful Orange County. How could I possibly go backwards to a life that didn't serve me?

When I told Gino this, it crushed him. It was painful to see such a powerful man slouch with defeat. His shoulders rounded forward and his eyes brimmed with tears. I couldn't bear to hurt him, but I know in my heart he was not the one for me.

At the end of the meal, I said goodbye to Gino forever and gave him a final hug. This time his body was stiffer and less affectionate as the cool night air swirled around us. Like the sun falling into night, the time for Gino was over.

> That night, I could feel a change happening in myself. I was no longer a victim of the men that surrounded me, that tried to control me.

By saying no to Gino I said yes to myself. I stood more strongly on my own two feet. I was growing up.

However, that didn't mean that the nightmare of Dave had gone from my memory. In fact, it still haunted me. In little moments when I least expected it, Dave came back to me. In an attempt to never feel the pain of rape again, I repressed every good or bad feeling. It made me a ticking time bomb of sorts, teetering on the edge of an inevitable explosion.

I soon learned that any time I was intimate with another man the trauma of Dave would resurface. One particular instance, I had started dating Dan, a man I had met through a friend of a friend. Dan and I were very passionate and in the heat of a summer day, we were rolling around, flinging our clothes in opposite directions. As the intensity rose, so did the feelings of anger, shame, and disgust I felt within myself. In a flash, I opened my eyes to see Dave on top of me instead of Dan, and I shrieked in horror. I slapped him furiously, pulled my pants back over my legs and ran.

My life in California was dwindling. I had been in Laguna for eight years and I was ready for something new. While I loved my job at the boutique, it became increasingly difficult to keep my head above water financially, as rent prices on the West Coast soared. I was homesick for my family, especially my sister.

As the seasons changed in 1992, I knew my next big step was to head back home to Milwaukee.

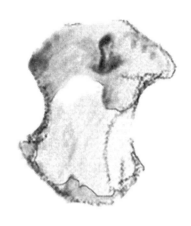

CHAPTER 6

MOVING BACK TO MY ROOTS

"I forgive and totally release the past and all past experiences, and I am free". - Louise Hay

AFTER EIGHT LONG years in California, it was time for a change. I felt homesick for my former Midwestern life. I longed for the culture where strangers were kind and said hello on the streets. California had no doubt been good to me. It had provided valuable lessons, both in my personal and professional life. But the expenses of living and working there were adding up, and I felt like I would never be able to grab a foothold financially.

I hadn't been back to Milwaukee in thirteen years. I filled up a trailer of all my possessions, shipped my car across the country, and said goodbye to a few dear friends. I didn't hesitate in these final moments, I knew in my heart it was time to return

Returning to my parent's home in Wisconsin inevitably unearthed the raw pain associated with the trauma that had occurred there.

I knew at some point I needed to face the demons head-on that plagued me or else I would never be free from them.

Perhaps it was female intuition that led me back to this reconciliation so many years later. I didn't know how to heal entirely, but I knew moving home seemed like a logical place to start.

Once again, the world was open for me to decide what chapter was to be written next. It was both exciting and unnerving. I had experienced many different lives since my departure at nineteen, and I was returning a new woman. It felt both comforting and uncomfortable at once.

Soon after I was back home, I decided to attend massage school, because healing others was always something that came naturally to me. As I grew up, I learned of the many forms this could take in my life. Sometimes it was as simple as comforting a friend in a time of need, or helping women select clothes while working in retail. In whatever job I chose, at any given time, I felt a deep, profound connection to others and a passion for helping them.

Friends have told me all my life that I should of been a therapist, because I always gave great advice. I have lived so much life and experienced so fully, that I can relate to pretty much anyone and understand them. While listening to others problems professionally sounded daunting, I used my gift of healing almost daily in my social circles. This curiosity led me to study massage, so I could assist others and heal their bodies with my touch.

Once I decided to go back to school to study massage, my parents agreed to help me. They offered to let me live at home and wouldn't charge me rent as long as I was pursuing school. This was just the support I needed, but I thought I might as well get an easy part-time job for some side money while I was studying.

While I was nostalgic and happy to be back, I felt completely detached from anyone or anything in Wisconsin. Any friends I had in the area had either moved away or had families and homes on their own. Over the years—and in an age before the internet—I had lost touch. I thought a job that would reconnect me to the community would be ideal. Once I knew this goal I found the most perfect job! It was working at Bradley Center—a huge stadium venue that held various concerts and games throughout the year. I would be a supervisor at the suite level, a perfect position to meet new people.

Between my job and school work, I began to adjust back to life back home. However in my quiet alone moments, the trauma of Dave would often resurface. I decided the next logical thing to do for my healing was to tell my parents the story of what had happened to me that day.

I decided to tell them separately, as I wanted complete privacy. I chose my mother first, because I felt more comfortable discussing it with a female figure. We were alone in the kitchen shortly after I had moved back into her home. I was helping her unload some groceries. We were deep in conversation about the life I used to have here, about how much she missed me when I had left. A window opened up in the conversation, and I considered it fate. When the moment was right, I stopped unloading groceries, placed my hand on my mother's hand to emphasize the weight of the moment. I looked in her in her lovely light blue eyes and told her that Dave had raped me.

My mother was visibly saddened. We cried for a few moments together, feeling the common thread we possessed between mother and daughter, and the pain that was mutual between us.

Mom retold the last few months of my relationship with Dave, and it was utterly surreal to hear her perspective. I had been so consumed in my own life at the time; I hadn't even considered her experience. Mom told me she knew that something had happened to me, something terrible. She described how bitter and cold I seemed, how unaffectionate, and somewhat traumatized. After a while it was too hard to hear so we stopped talking and just cried. And, when the crying felt enough, we stopped, hugged each other, restated our undying love and support of one another, then went back to unloading the groceries.

It proved more difficult to tell my father of the date rape. Talking about anything related to sex was always forbidden as a child, and that shame remained in adulthood. I couldn't imagine what it would feel like as a father, knowing something so traumatic had happened to your little girl.

For whatever reason, I knew that telling Dad the truth was a crucial step for my recovery, so I followed through. I found a quiet moment when he was watching television late at night. Between commercials, I grabbed the remote, turned down the TV and told my dad that I had been date raped by Dave at eighteen. He was quieter than my mother, but still agreed that he had noticed a difference in me. He painted a similar picture—me as a sullen, withdrawn teen that had clearly been suffering. He extended all the compassion and sincerity in the world to me. He fought back tears a few times, but mostly our exchange brief and to the point.

Afterwards, I walked down the hallway and went to bed. Lying in my childhood bedroom sent a wave of memories into my mind. Reliving the date rape had been excruciatingly painful on many levels.

But somewhere in my heart

I knew that it was necessary for me to heal from the trauma that had occurred.

And, having coached my friends and family through the process of healing for themselves, I trusted my intuition and followed where it was taking me.

The last step in my process of forgiveness, and probably the hardest, was to forgive Dave for what he had done to me. I feel that if you don't forgive someone you only hold resentment and or vengeance in your heart.

As the saying goes…

"LET GO, LET GOD."

While it seemed insurmountable, I knew it must be done. One day I found myself alone in the house when my parents took a trip together for the weekend. In the emptiness of my former home, I began to feel strong enough to walk into the guest room by the garage where it had happened. Instantly my knees buckled and I fell to the floor.

Life Interrupted

The memory of Dave overtook me. I recalled our entire relationship as I sobbed big messy tears into the sleeve of my sweater. Each picture of Dave that came into my mind caused a bigger fit of tears, each one rolling over me like a wave. I thought of the first second I laid eyes on him, the initial attraction that I felt. My heart poured with emotions. I was all at once shameful and guilty but also terribly tired of feeling those things.

On the deepest levels of my soul I wanted freedom most of all, freedom from the prison that Dave had kept me in without even knowing.

When I was tired of remembering Dave, and recalling the rape that occurred in vivid detail, I decided to forgive him. Though it seemed impossible, I knew in my heart that true forgiveness was the key to healing.

I reached deep within myself and dug for a rationale for forgiveness. Dave was young, I thought, we both were. Maybe Dave didn't know any better. Maybe he was on a spiritual journey just like everyone else. It was difficult to do, but the longer I sat, cried, and extended my best version of forgiveness, I could feel the weight lifting.

I told Dave aloud that I would forgive him but not forget. There is a huge difference. It was a humbling process to find the forgiveness, but there was also no way I could undo the damage he had done. Much like the scars on our skin, trauma will fade with time, but the deepest ones will be known forever.

My past is who I am. I have learned to accept this and move forward in spite of—and because of—the unfolding that has happened in my life. I hope to help and inspire women that might have experienced something like I have. If that's you, I hope you know there is hope for you. I sincerely want to extend the gift of hope to any woman who is suffering.

***

All in all, after I had adjusted, cried, and forgiven, my life back in Milwaukee was happy. My relationship with my parents took on a new form after we had discussed what had happened with Dave. It felt more open and honest than ever before, and in my older age I was able to relate to them as an adult and not an angry teenager. I guess I hadn't realized that my connection with them was also in need of repair.

I continued to focus on massage school, and work at The Bradley Center part time. Things felt balanced for the first time in a while. My job was also fun, and surrounded me with young and exuberant friends to connect with.

And then came Mary—an outgoing boisterous blonde who quickly became my friend. Mary and I shared many shifts together, and would spend most of the time laughing and conversing. She was always outgoing and willing to listen. She was my first new friend since I returned back home and she was exactly what I needed: the perfect antidote to the heaviness of my past.

One night after our shifts, Mary asked if I would join her for a drink at a nearby Italian spot. I resisted big time. I wanted to be home at a reasonable hour, mostly to connect with my parents over dinner and then get a good night's sleep for a full day of school tomorrow. Mary insisted. She was already putting on lipstick and earrings. Sometimes she wouldn't take no for an answer. Finally I agreed to just "one drink" mostly just to shut her up.

In my heart, though, I wasn't ready to meet anyone. I was still reeling from the weirdness of the last few years, the painful journey I had taken away from home and back.

Mary and I situated ourselves at Lucci's Restaurant on Water Street. We shared a bottle of Merlot. Mary immediately hopped out of her seat when she noticed three men who entered the bar. She gave enthusiastic hugs and introduced one of them to me as Todd Durand.

Todd introduced himself to me and I immediately noticed his piercing blue eyes and mess of chestnut hair. We spoke about twenty minutes just of pleasantries and light conversation. I had no desire of getting involved in a relationship, but I went with it.

After the last drop of wine disappeared from my glass, I said my goodbyes to Todd, gave Mary a squeeze as I left, and slipped out.

The next day at work, Mary grilled me about Todd. She heard that he had asked for my number through another employee and I had refused. Mary insisted that I give him my number. My reaction was immediate and blunt. "I don't give my number out." But Mary, as usual, didn't take no for an answer.

"Come on Lu," she begged. "He's such a nice guy!"

Once again I caved to Mary's persistence. I agreed that Todd could have my number, but I never expected him to use it. I was surprised when my parent's phone rang later that evening. His voice on the other end sounded calm and soothing. Before I realized, an hour and a half had passed. Todd and I agreed to talk again the following night.

It was mid-September 1991. Todd and I spoke almost every evening for the rest of month. We grew to know each other over the phone, and I looked forward to our daily exchange.

I spent two months talking to him off and on, and then, coincidentally, I spent a full week in Paris during November—a trip that was a gift from my sister, and one we had been planning for months, I'm sure if the timing was better we would of already had our first date by now, but it was almost refreshing talking for as long as we did and starting a friendship first.

Of course when I was abroad I didn't speak to Todd. These were the days of long distance connections, no wifi, and still, he was brand new in my life. But undeniably the air of Paris overtook me when I was there. I walked through the Champs-Elysees and reminisced about him.

When I returned, full of cheese, bread, and love that Paris has a way of doing, Todd and I had set a date for December

10th. It was the first time we would both be available, and it was long overdue.

What's really strange is I had somehow planned another date with an engineer for that afternoon. It was a setup that a friend had insisted I meet, and for some strange fate, it landed exactly on the same day I had planned to meet Todd, also an engineer.

The first date was mediocre at best. I felt no real connection talking to him, and when it was over I was so bored I just wanted to leave. I went back to my parent's house to recuperate, and by the time I did, it was already time to go again.

While my feet dragged to meet Todd, by the time I saw him, I was glad I had taken the risk. He was so much more striking than I had remembered. Tall, muscular, with shiny medium brown hair and disarming blue eyes, he resembled both Richard Gere and Patrick Swayze.

My father greeted Todd first, and when he did he was wearing toupee to cover his receding hairline. Todd shook my father's hand so hard the toupee fell off! Poor Todd, he didn't know what to say, but luckily my dad was laughing loudly. I could tell they liked each other immediately.

To avoid more embarrassment, I escorted Todd to the living room to have a seat as I disappeared into the kitchen to make him a drink.

As soon as my mother got a look at him, she hurried into the kitchen behind me.

"Lu!" she exclaimed in a hushed voice. "Whatever you do, don't fuck this one up!"

This coming from my Catholic mother who never swears.

"Oh mom!" I exclaimed. "You just want me married!"

I served the drinks and Todd and I chatted lightly about travel. He was so compelling and easy to talk to; I felt relaxed and happy in his company. Then we left and drove to a restaurant called Fox and Hounds—a quiet and romantic spot.

Dinner lasted a few hours. We were so comfortable with each other and everything felt effortless and exciting. At one point the waitress interrupted and asked if we were celebrating our engagement. We both laughed at the thought!

As dinner was winding down, I cut to the chase.

"Ok let's just get this over with, could you just kiss me?"

You know, if the kiss isn't right, nothing is! And, at thirty-two, I definitely knew what I wanted. I knew then after so many relationships what I was and wasn't looking for in a man. After such an engaging conversation, I wanted to be sure to show my interest. Todd was a bit taken aback by my directness, but he agreed. As soon as he kissed me, I never wanted to stop...And I didn't.

Our relationship continued to unfold. I knew within six months Todd was the one for me. He was truly an unexpected blessing. I knew it in my heart and I still know it every day that I look at him. Todd is kind, strong, a devoted father, and endlessly loving. He is my companion through life, my soul mate. Through all of the pain and suffering that men have caused me, Todd is my reminder that there is always a reason for heartbreak. Todd is proof that through every interruption, God is always guiding you to realize the highest truth.

Life Interrupted

GOD'S PLAN FOR YOUR MATE

Everyone longs to give himself completely to someone: to have a deep soul relationship with another; to be loved thoroughly and exclusively. However, God to a Christian says, no, not until you are satisfied, fulfilled, and content with being loved by me, alone. With giving yourself totally and unreservedly to Me. To having an intensely personal and unique relationship with Me, alone. Discovering that only in Me is your satisfaction to be found, will you be capable of the perfect human relationship that I plan for you.

You will never be united with another until you are united with Me, really united with another, exclusive of anyone, or anything else, exclusive of any other desires or longings. I want you to stop planning, stop wishing, and allow Me to give you the most thrilling plan existing...one that you cannot imagine.

I want you to have the best, please allow Me to bring it to you. Just keep watching Me... expecting the greatest things. Keep experiencing the satisfaction that I Am. And keep listening and learning the things I tell you.

You just wait, that's all...wait. Don't be anxious, don't worry, don't look around at the things that others have gotten or I have given them. Don't look at the things you think you want. Just keep on looking off and away to Me, or you will miss what I want to show you. And then, when you are ready, I'll surprise you with a love far more wonderful than anything you would dream of.

You see, until you are ready and until the one I have for you is ready, and I am working even at this moment to have both of you ready at the same time. Until you are both satisfied exclusively with me and the life I prepare for you, you won't be able to experience the love that exemplifies your relationship with Me. And this is perfect love. And, dear one, I want you to have the most wonderful love.

I want to see in you, in the flesh a picture of your relationship with Me. And, I want you to enjoy materially, the everlasting union and beauty and perfection and love that I offer you with Myself. I know that I love you utterly. I am El Shaddai-most loving Father, God Almighty. Believe it and be satisfied and I will satisfy you.

- Author unknown

Life Interrupted

We married in 1995, after three and a half years together. About a year after we were married, my Grandfather fell sick and I went to visit him in the hospital. While I stood at his bedside, I knew it may be the last time I would get to speak to him. I cherished it. Grandpa took my hand in his and looked straight into my eyes. As I looked back, I imagined all the life he had lived. I felt immense gratitude and compassion for his journey into heaven. He was leaving behind a life full of love and purpose.

"A little bird told me a secret." Grandpa whispered with a playful tone. "Someone is having a baby boy."

He gestured vaguely to my stomach and I was shocked.

"What are you talking about?" I said with disbelief. "No way I am pregnant!"

On that same weekend, I realized I had missed my period. Panicked, I drove to the drugstore to buy a pregnancy test. Todd was working and I had the day off. I was watching Days of our Lives, and on the commercial break, I ran to the bathroom to test myself. Before my show came back on the TV, almost instantly, the test turned a glaring positive result.

My first instinct was complete terror. Then after a few moments to collect myself, I decided I would deliver the news to Todd that evening when he arrived home from work. Oddly enough, it was right after our first wedding anniversary. As newlyweds, we mutually decided that we didn't need gifts; we were happy just spending a quiet evening together. So when Todd walked into a romantic dinner with candles, he was shocked. I played it cool.

"Just something I threw together last minute" I assured him, my hands shaking as I served the wine I would only pretend to drink.

Once dinner was ending, I could barely contain myself anymore. I handed Todd a card with a handwritten message. I watched anxiously as he opened it across from me, eyes welling with tears. I wrote:

"Will you be my husband…?

…My lover…

…And the father of our child to be?"

Todd agreed, and we were overjoyed. We held each other all night wiping away tears of joy.

Unfortunately, my Grandfather died just before our first son Austin was born. I still never knew how my Grandpa knew I was pregnant with a boy, but I am convinced it was a message straight from God.

Life Interrupted

CHAPTER 7

THE CARDINAL MESSAGE

"Having a relationship with God comes all answers, solutions, healings, and all new creations which in turn opens endless doors of opportunities"

I ALWAYS SAID THAT I wanted to have my children three and a half years apart. I guess God was listening because when Austin was about three, I noticed some irregular spotting and went to the doctor. Sure enough, I was pregnant—

something happily unplanned but joyfully welcomed by both Todd and me. We were delighted to grow our family. However, the spotting was concerning to my gynecologist, and she suggested I come in for regular blood work to be sure the baby was healthy. Over the next few weeks, the medical staff monitored my alpha-beta proteins, which should increase as a fetus develops. At my fourth week, my alpha-betas exploded, registering in the thousands. The nurse who took my blood furrowed her brows and looked over her clipboard, "Are you expecting twins?" she asked.

I laughed at the thought. Twins seemed like a handful and I was sure I wanted only one baby.

At my seventh week of pregnancy, we flew to Naples, Florida. Todd's brother was getting married and we were excited to celebrate. I was playing in the pool with Austin, who was still a toddler, when, out of nowhere, I felt a huge gush in my swimsuit. At first, I thought I had peed my pants! I handed Austin to Todd and rushed to the bathroom. My intuition was screaming at full volume that something had gone terribly wrong.

I peeled off my wet swimsuit to reveal gobs of blood between my legs. A stream of blood and fluid fell into the toilet as I watched, horrified. Through the murky water, I could make out a small sack. I was absolutely sure I had a miscarriage and began shrieking for Todd. Blood was still pouring out of me endlessly. Todd arrived and calmly dialed 911. Shortly after, an ambulance came to take me to the emergency room. Todd held me as I shook and cried. I knew I had lost our baby.

At the Naples Hospital, my bladder was filled with water to facilitate an ultrasound. The experience was excruciatingly painful—both physically and emotionally. Though I had gone through labor with my first son, Austin, this pain was nearly tripled, not to mention the complete devastation of losing a baby. Still, I remained vigilant. I trusted that God had a bigger plan.

In the ER, I met Dr. Fransi, a kind, soft-spoken French man who performed my ultrasound. Together we gazed at a murky illuminated screen and analyzed the situation. In the center of the screen, I saw a small black mass.

"What's that?" I asked.

Dr. Fransi looked at me with optimism in his kind eyes.

"That's your baby," he whispered.

Then something remarkable happened. The doctor spoke to me, but he didn't use any words. He was looking at me, his blue eyes piercing deep into my soul, and he telepathically assured me my baby would be healthy. I heard the most beautiful and truthful voice fill my mind with positive reassurance. My heart filled with joy. I knew my baby boy would live.

What happened to me is fairly common among pregnancies. Nick had a twin (sometimes called a "ghost twin"), that died in the womb in the first precious weeks, but Nick survived. The partial miscarriage had left behind a large amount of blood in my uterus that would either pull baby Nick out of me or gently reabsorb into my body. Though I was shaken, I knew the outcome would be the latter. I knew after hearing the telepathic message that everything would be ok.

On December 21st, 2000, Todd had left for a work conference in Boston. Our baby wasn't due for another month, so I felt comfortable staying home alone. That night around four am, I woke up to discover that I was laying in a pool of fluid. Immediately I feared something had gone wrong; it seemed much too early for our baby boy to arrive. I called the doctor who told me to stay put and relax, it could be nothing.

"Sit down and rest," she said. "If you keep releasing fluid, come into the hospital and we'll examine you."

She was almost too calm. My intuition spoke up again— like it has all my life. Though I was afraid, it told me to stay calm and to keep faith. I sat upright in my bedroom and felt my insides churning into twisted knots. The sun was just beginning to lighten the night sky with a rosy shade of pink. A new day was a beginning and maybe a new life. My baby had a divine plan, that much was clear. He was excited to come forward into the world, to bring his gifts, and to experience the fullness of life. That gave me happiness through the fear. I could feel Nick's wish to be born in the deepest parts of my heart.

I kept releasing fluid, so I called my sister. Luckily, my parents—being the true "snowbirds"— had just flocked to Florida at the first signs of winter's chill. I called them as soon as I hung up with my sister. They agreed to watch Austin at home while my sister took me to the hospital.

Within hours of arriving at the hospital, I was in full-blown labor. Though it felt strange without Todd, I didn't want to interfere with Mother Nature's plan. Nick was arriving whether or not we were ready, and we all felt blessed all the same. My sister was in the delivery room and took lots of pictures. Because she had never maternally given birth, it felt extra meaningful to have her by my side.

At 8:50 am Nick came into the world, and by 2:30 that afternoon, I was feeling well enough to walk around and celebrate. At 8:30 pm, Todd burst through the doors of the hospital room, looking exhausted and ecstatic. His trip from Boston had been delayed because of snow. He had only made it as far as Chicago when he heard news of my labor. He made some friends at the airport that were also headed to Milwaukee and together they rented a limo. He had driven all night through the snow with strangers!

Todd rushed in and embraced me and our new son. We laughed about what a chaotic journey it had been to finally hold our beautiful new baby.

It had been nothing but interruptions, but it had all been worth it."

When Nick was about six years old, I became interested in Reiki—a spiritual technique that uses life force through the hands to promote healing. I found a teacher, Claire, and during one of our lessons, she began talking about the healing powers of crystals. She opened a case full of stones and had me select one that spoke to me. I looked over the crystals and picked a tiger's eye—a deep, amber colored stone that had distinctive orange stripes.

Claire's eyes widened when she saw the stone I had chosen.

"Tiger's Eye," she said, "is ideal for processing unresolved anger that may be locked in your soul."

That evening, I went home wearing the Tiger's Eye around my neck. I had told my teacher nothing of my life that would indicate I needed the stone, but somehow she knew. It was remarkable that I chose exactly the stone I had needed for myself.

At home, Nick noticed my new necklace right away; he was drawn to it. He sat in my lap and gazed deeply into the stone, examining its fluorescent stripes and glossy finish.

"I want one too, Mama!" he exclaimed.

This surprised me. What six-year-old boy do you know wants a necklace? But I knew something deeper was at play here. There was something spiritual calling Nick to find his own crystal, and I didn't take that lightly. I told him tomorrow we could visit the shop and he could pick his own.

The next day, Nick peered over the same case that I had, taking in all the glittering stones below him. He playfully picked them up and examined them. He asked lots of questions and was full of energy. When it came time to choose, Nick settled on a pink quartz. It was small, no more than two inches long, with a narrow point at the end. Claire clasped it around his neck and he swelled with pride.

It was the height of summer in Florida and the heat was unrelenting. As soon as Nick and I returned home from our crystal excursion, he wanted to jump in the pool. I took my usual post in the oversized lawn chair that sat adjacent to our pool and helped him change into his swimsuit. Just before he was about to dive in, I reminded him to take off the necklace. I told him to set it on the glass table that was situated just behind me.

Just as Nick gently tapped the tip of the stone on to the glass table it shattered. I'll never forget the sound it made—both beautiful and haunting—as a million fragments of sun-filled glass released onto our patio, each one making a high-pitched "tink!" as it struck the earth with energetic fervor.

Then the pieces assembled into a pile where the table once stood as if some invisible force was connecting them all back together again. Though we dug through the pile, Nick's necklace was completely gone.

When I called my teacher to ask about what had happened, she asked what year Nick had been born. I told her it was 2000, and that he was a millennium baby.

"Oh," her voice murmured softly, "a star child! He has been given many gifts, this child. He clearly came forth with energy, intention, and passion. He has a lot to release and looks like he found a way to do so!"

No kidding, I thought. Nick was and still is a very special child. He holds a life-affirming spirit and a generous heart. He is a star child that continues to give many special gifts.

My family is the one I have always wanted. As the years rolled by and the seasons passed, I melted into my life of joy. For everything that had traumatized me in the first half of life, the second half was making up for it tenfold.

That isn't to say my adulthood was entirely smooth sailing. With the years that came after starting a family, more interruptions followed. Many more.

I continue to believe that through every dark moment in life, through every experience that makes you feel like caving in and giving up, there is a deep and true spiritual lesson to be realized. Our pain is our gain, so to speak. In each defeat, an opportunity to evolve more into the highest version of you inevitably comes forth.

In early 2006, just as the hazy remnants of a Florida winter drifted from the tropical skies, the ease and perfection of life was sharply interrupted. This time it came in the form of a phone call. My mother's unmistakable voice—shaken with despair—spoke on the other end.

"Lu, I have some bad news…"

Immediately, I knew this news was about my father. Call it my powerful intuition, or simply by the tone of my mother's voice, either way, I knew. Unfortunately, this wasn't the first time I've heard my mother speak this way, as my father had been sick many times throughout my life. His poor health at times felt like a precarious situation ready to topple. I underestimated how strong my mother was back then: raising us every day, keeping our spirits light and our family together, never knowing when my Dad's emergency trip to the hospital may be his last.

Fortunately, though, my father was tough as a bull. He never complained. He rose at dawn every morning in my childhood and worked a long day complete with the genuine admiration and companionship of his coworkers. Dad had many deep friendships, and his genuine love of people set him apart. It was almost as if the love and happiness he gave to others made him strong enough to conquer any physical limitations that life happened to deal him.

"I think you and Todd ought to come back," Mom said quietly on the other line of the telephone, "one last time."

Dad had been in the hospital due to thyroid cancer. It all happened so quickly. He had been steadily chugging through life when he happened to cough up blood one day. Because he had always had sinus issues (not to mention his blood disorder, poor circulation, and other complications), the doctors did not quickly dismiss him. They decided to do a CT scan from the chest and upward instead of one just of the sinuses, and thank God they did.

Closer investigation had revealed that Dad had two goiters that had grown so oddly—wrapped around his collarbone—they were almost impossible to detect and delicate to operate on. In the smaller of the two, doctors found cancer. When they attempted to remove it, Dad bled out, a symptom of his blood disorder that made him an extremely dangerous risk. The hospital staff concluded there was nothing else they could do. Radiation was also used a few times, but that too created internal bleeding for my dad. At this point, the medical team had only one remaining suggestion: enjoy what was left of his life.

Todd and I flew back that evening. We had just visited a few weeks ago before Dad underwent the surgery that proved to be ineffective. The last few months had been fraught with uncertainty. My dad was such an important figure to me, and I couldn't imagine the enormous void my life would become without him. He meant everything to me: a leader, a role model, an irreplaceable grandfather to my boys. He always had jovial and positive attitude, and a shoulder to cry on. He would always pick up the phone with an enthusiastic "Bonjourno! Hey kiddo what's shaken?" His friends even coined him the nickname, "Johnny Bonjourno."

Needless to say, it took all my strength not to totally collapse under the weight of losing him.

When Todd and I arrived at the hospital, I could feel the energetic heaviness as I walked through the automatic glass doors at the entrance. Already something very existential and powerful was expecting me that day. I clenched Todd's elbow as we approached my father's room.

The entire family (my sister, brothers, sister-in-laws, Mom, Todd, and I) huddled around Dad. I was situated at his feet, massaging them softly as I spoke my final words to him. My thumbs moved in tiny circles over and over again into the soles of his feet, which were limp and heavy from the morphine that was dripping in his IV. In the corner, a robotic beep sounded from his heart monitor. The morphine and heart monitor were the only things between Dad and Heaven.

Throughout my father's final moments on earth, I was having intense out-of-body experiences. The entire hospital room appeared to me in an altered state of reality, a different level of consciousness. The end of life was so near to someone we all loved, and through our synergy, a divine shift was occurring.

Physically, I felt myself at the foot of my father's bed, sobbing and holding onto him with shaking hands. Then, for a few minutes at a time, I was no longer physical at all. I saw the entire scene from a broader perspective, almost as if I was hovering on the ceiling watching from below. These episodes continued for a few hours. Given the intensity of the situation, I told no one of my experience.

It was surreal to see various friendships from Dad's illustrious life come forth to wish him well in the afterlife. His passion for connecting with others and maintaining substantial relationships couldn't be overlooked. It was moving, joyous, and sad—the grand finale of a life of love and service. It was obvious the impact he had had on everyone he encountered.

On some level, my Dad knew it was his time to go. That reassured me in a way. My out-of-body experiences were getting longer and more intense. The doctors entered to report that they were ending my father's maintenance medication. His breathing began to close, it was at this time they turned off the machine. My father then took his last breath and it was time to say goodbye.

It was around 12 pm on June 6th, 2007. I had returned to my position at my Dad's feet. He had always enjoyed my massages, and it felt fitting for me to be using my gift—my healing touch—as Dad slipped away. Then suddenly, I felt Dad go. Just as he gasped his final breath on earth, a shudder of air rushed through my entire body, starting in my hands where I was holding him and up through my chest and out. It was painful. It reminded me of that scene in "Ghost" with Patrick Swayze. The soul of my father had traveled through me as it exited life in pursuit of Heaven.

Todd had been standing directly behind me when it happened. After Dad passed, Todd respectfully turned for the door to give my mother and siblings some privacy in their grief. When I saw Todd leave I left too. My father was gone and all that remained was an empty shell.

In the hallway, I asked Todd if he had felt my father exit. There was really no other way to phrase it. Undeniably something spiritual and tangible had occurred, and I knew it whether or not Todd had experienced it too. But the weird thing was that he *had.*

"Yes," Todd confirmed, even before I had finished asking the question. "Your father left through our bodies...and it *hurt.*"

With that, I had all the reassurance I needed. I returned to the hospital room. My final wish was that Dad would be safe and at peace with God in Heaven. I whispered in his ear my final "I love you," and one request:

"When you find Heaven, come and tell me in my dreams".

Life Interrupted

CHAPTER 8

EXPECT THE UNEXPECTED

"I used to think God guided us by opening and closing doors, but now I know sometimes God wants us to kick some doors down."— Bob Goff

CATHOLICISM WAS THE mainstay of religion in my family growing up. As Midwesterners, faith was a cornerstone in our values, both as a community and individually. Faith was a pillar in our home. We attended church every Sunday and attended bible school. As children we were taught repeatedly about sins, evil, and redemption.

As I grew into an adult, Catholic ideas seemed far too black and white for me. What about the broad subjectivity of sin? What about all of the shades of gray that exist within right and wrong? These questions arose frequently as I grew into maturity.

Ever the curious one, I took it upon myself to research religion in an attempt to think for myself. Everything I read and explored on the topic fascinated me: life, death, rebirth, sin, forgiveness, God. In my searching, I came to a deeper and more significant understanding of my place in the Universe and how to live in harmony with God.

In my searching for truth, I researched a few Buddhist texts. I came across the concept of the soul exiting the body in the time of death. Buddhists believe, like many religions, that the body is merely a physical vessel that carries the soul which is eternal. What's interesting is that Buddhists also believe that the soul exits the body through the top of the head if they are ready to pass, and down through the feet if they are not ready and resisting the change. It makes sense when you figure that the head of the body, which houses the brain and by extension the mind, is the highest place of a human, both spiritually and physically. The feet, in contrast, are the lowest body part and the most connected to the physical aspect of being on Earth.

It was clear to me that Dad wasn't ready to leave. I know that he resisted the inevitable. I could feel his resistance even when he was alive. He struggled with death the way he struggled most of his life, fighting to stay alive. But in the end, I believe my Dad's death was a way for him to finally stop fighting and start letting go...

(All his life, I joked because he was like a cute Buddha. He sure had the cute belly to match. I would joke with him, rubbing his protruding stomach and say, "I wish, I wish, I wish!" He hated that, of course.)

Though my father and I differed in our religious beliefs, I still believe he guided me to finding my gift of healing. Because he was occasionally sick from his illness or exhausted from working, I would often massage him to alleviate the dull achiness and skin ulcers that life caused him. This strengthened our bond, and allowed me to realize my full potential.

Life Interrupted

When I was studying in massage school, our graduating assignment was to find a person who could benefit from weekly massage therapy and record their progress. Naturally my father fit the bill, so we had a regularly scheduled massage hour every week which we would both look forward to. He especially needed relief from the varicose ulcers in his legs, something I knew I could heal with regular therapy.

One afternoon, Dad and I were alone in the house during our massage appointment. Like usual, he had fallen asleep on my table, and the faint noise of his snoring broke the silence. I didn't mind that he slept, it allowed me to focus even more intensely on my gift, and it made me laugh when he emerged from the table with a deep circular imprint around his face and his eyes heavy with relaxation.

As I worked through the stiff muscles on my father's legs, something very unusual happened. I had been focusing intensely on him for a long time, with all of my energy funneling into God's healing power through my touch. Then, I began to see faint traces of soft, white light emerge through my fingertips and channel into his body. The more I focused the more powerful and electric the light became. It was undeniably, God's healing power manifested. At one point, I turned my palms face up to examine them. The sight actually frightened me: bright white light, full of electricity emanated from my palms.

When he awoke, I searched my father's face for any recognition of what had occurred. He looked the same: groggy, relaxed, the tell-tale imprint of the massage table around his smiling face.

"Dad," I started, not knowing what to say. "Did you feel anything... *different* about this session?"

Dad looked confused. "No... should I?"

I stammered for a moment, it felt to utterly silly to explain to him what had happened, but I knew in my heart what I had felt.

"I saw a beautiful white light... come through my fingers and flow into your legs... "

He laughed before I could continue.

"Sure!" he said. "And next you'll be walking on water!"

My massage class was far more receptive to my story. I explained what had happened in great detail for my graduating project. I included the healing light I had felt emanating from my hands. My teacher was fascinated. She asked me if she could publish what I had written about my experience, but I declined. It didn't matter to me that people know or understand what had happened. I was just happy to make someone I love feel better.

More and more, I was obtaining the validation that massage was the right career choice for me, after so many other trials and tribulations. I knew I was put on this Earth to heal others. After venturing out one day while living in California, I found a "Healing Center" in Orange County. I walked inside not knowing what to expect. I was directed by a very sweet older woman to go through the first door to your right and have a seat; it will be just a minute. I entered the room sat down and in front of me sat two young women and one young man.

"You have quite the energy!" the young man said. "Do you realize that when you were born you came into this life with 85% healing capacity?"

I responded, "No, I had no idea..."

"Oh that's not all," the young man rose from his chair. "You also brought with you a huge congregation of angels, and priests, you sure are protected!"

***

Three months after my father died, he visited me in my dreams just as he said he would. One night, I dreamt I was shopping in the Wellington mall (of all places!). The mood around me was happy, peaceful and calm. My feet stepped onto the escalator and carried me downward to the first story of the mall. All around me, bright white marble glistened and yellow light gleamed from the stores and chandeliers.

At the bottom of the escalator, I saw my father. It was fitting—he loved the mall and was always a blast to take shopping. I valued his opinion on clothes and he generally had killer style and a good eye.

In my dream he looked wonderful: calm, present, happy, and joyous. He was wearing white linen pants and a loose yellow shirt that breezed effortlessly around his frame he walked towards me.

Having researched extensively about dream interpretations, I knew these colors were significant. White is a color of peace, truth, and spiritual divinity. Yellow represents joy, happiness, and forgiveness. I was thrilled to see him dressed this way, finally at peace after the struggle I felt him go through when he died.

The most striking thing though, was that my father's face was glowing. An unmistakable warmth radiated from deep within him. I knew this meant he was at peace.

When I stepped off the escalator and walked towards him, a rush of well-being and love filled my entire body. I embraced him warmly and felt his strong arms wrap around me. I wanted to cry but I was also so happy, and so relieved that he was safe. He spoke to me then, not aloud but through his mind. I heard his words without his mouth moving, without hearing a sound. Telepathically, he told me he made it; he was in Heaven.

And that was the last time I saw him.

"LIFE, AS I SEE IT"

Life Interrupted

CHAPTER 4

AWAKEN THE HEALING

"Never be a prisoner of your past, it was just a lesson not a life sentence." - Anonymous

IN THE MONTHS that followed my father's death, I processed the grief quietly. I retreated into myself, became a hermit of sorts, and unpacked the loss. Everyone processes trauma differently. My method was to mourn in silence and solitude.

After a few months, I realized that my period was missing. At first I disregarded it as the start of perimenopause or just plain stress, which can happen when trauma, loss, or sickness occurs. After all, I could feel the weight of my father's passing manifesting in my body. Maybe this was just a side effect?

When September came and still no period, I made an appointment with my gynecologist. He determined that I was perimenopausal, and recommended either going on the pill to regulate my body, hormone replacement or an endometrial ablation, a procedure that destroys (ablates) the uterine lining, or endometrium. This procedure is used to treat abnormal uterine bleeding. An ablation felt like the best way to go under the circumstances, I had already finished with childbearing, so I was an ideal candidate.

I agreed to the procedure and the required biopsy that must be done prior to it. I had the option of having it done at my doctor's office or the hospital. Because the hospital required anesthesia, I decided the office, only because it seemed like the easier option. I had no reason to be nervous. I never had a biopsy come back unusual, and this one was no exception. Everything came out great. I went home to rest in preparation for the ablation to be done in a few days.

That night I had a dream. I heard a male voice, the most beautiful and loving voice I've ever heard, but firm and commanding. I truly believe God was speaking to me. With immense kindness and severity, he told me to have the procedure done at the hospital and not at the office as I had chosen. I felt his message echo through me in that instant.

When I awoke, I knew that God had spoken to me. I then told my husband, Todd, and he replied, "Your intuition has never steered you wrong. I support whatever you feel is best."

The next day I called the doctor and asked to do the procedure at the hospital.

I said, "Doc, I know you may think this is weird but I had an extremely vivid dream last night and a voice spoke to me and insisted I have my procedure done in the hospital."

The doctor replied, "I don't think it's weird, you need to be comfortable with whatever you decide is right for you."

I thought again about the voice that had visited me. As I recalled the dream, the voice, and the emotions, I shivered with goose bumps. For the first time, I thought the voice could have been my father. Maybe he was warning me about the procedure and manifesting into my dreams. I closed my eyes and went back into the dream. No, I was absolutely sure. The voice talking to me was God.

I've often had lucid dreams and been delivered divine guidance through them. For much of my life though, I didn't always know what or who was speaking to me, or why. I often reflect on the times I've followed the advice I've received in my dreams, and the times I did the exact opposite out of spite, bitterness, or distrust in the guidance being delivered. My diagnosis was the turning point in which I started to heed the words that were being spoken to me, and recognized them as the words of a higher power. Little did I know, this was only the beginning of a deeper and stronger relationship with God.

This was in October of 2007. Ten years later, the dream proved to speak the truth. I stumbled upon further research on the subject of uterine ablation surgery. The majority of these procedures had been performed incorrectly at a doctor's offices, like mine would have been. Sometimes they were even done without an anesthesiologist; I am so very thankful I followed that voice that was so beautiful but firm.

I found numerous reports of women who had undergone this and suffered major complications. Some had even died. Though I've known it all along, I further confirmed that God had saved my life in the moment he told me to have the ablation at the hospital.

When the day of the surgery arrived, Todd drove me to the hospital. We were quiet in the car. I could feel the tension of the moment, heavy with uncertainty, vibrating between us. We pulled up to the hospital and I felt slightly dizzy. I had been so healthy my whole life, being a patient was new and scary. Todd was supportive but I could feel his fear.

At the outpatient hospital, I was escorted to a room with outdated decor and gaudy curtains. It was divided into five sections. There were five other women who looked like they were around the same age as me and were to have ablations that same day. I later found out they were all having the same procedure by my doctor as well. Though I was nervous, I prayed to myself as I stared at the ceiling. I prayed that God would watch over me and guide the doctor to remove what is necessary and renew my healthy body.

Because I had chosen the hospital, the ablation consisted of something called dilation and curettage (D and C). This consists of a widening (dilation) of the lower part of the uterus (or cervix) to allow the doctor to insert an instrument; and then curettage: scraping of the uterus walls with a long, spoon-shaped instrument, also called curette. The tissue sample is then sent to the lab for examination.

If I would have chosen the doctor's office for this procedure, I would have missed this crucial step. What would have happened to me if I didn't have the D and C done? That I do not know, but I knew I needed to take charge and go with my intuition as it was voiced to me in my dream.

I got a call from my doctor the next day. I was standing in my bedroom. I heard the phone ring and picked it up. The doctor introduced himself on the line; I knew the news wasn't good. He calmly asked for me to come to the office, and my heart sank to my stomach. My vision tunneled and my body grew heavy and weak. I gasped for air. Todd came in and rushed to my side. He held me and tried to make sense through my sobbing. I knew it immediately: I knew I had cancer.

I arrived again at the doctor's office, this time heavy with fear. As the sliding doors glided open, Todd took my hand. A pang of fear and sadness shuttered through my body. Life's interruptions are like that. You never know when life might change. This moment is all we have; the future is never guaranteed. I thought about my life in an instant—about growing up, becoming an adult, having a family, it all felt surreal and overwhelming that it might end.

The doctor read my results and all my fears were confirmed. I had adenocarcinoma, a five millimeter malignant tumor formed from glandular structures in the epithelial tissue. He delivered this news with professionalism and sadness. I searched his face for hope, but couldn't find any.

I couldn't really accept that I had cancer. In fact, he mentioned that three of the five women that day came back with positive results. What if there had been a mistake?

"It's unlikely," the doctor said, "I even double-checked the results myself."

Todd and I drove home in complete silence. We were even quieter than before. My mind was racing. I really didn't believe I had cancer. What if the tests got switched by mistake? I knew it was unlikely, but things happen. How could I have cancer? I had none of the signs and symptoms. I was not at risk for this type of uterine cancer.

Todd parked the car in our driveway and stared out the window. We hadn't said a word to each other. I looked at him and felt his pain. I felt physical pain too, deep in my uterus from the ablation. I cupped my hands over my pelvis and winced in pain. The doctor's suggestion was to do a complete hysterectomy. I couldn't believe that after all this—the ablation, cancer, and the emotional loss of my father's passing, and now I'd have to wait six more weeks to heal and then have a major surgery and be cut open again! It was a bigger interruption than I had even imagined.

To comfort myself, I called my dear friend Katherine. In times of trauma, sometimes a good friend that has healing massage hands is just what I needed! Katherine is an expert body and energy worker, and she agreed to do some treatments on me with my new diagnosis.

There is something else special about Katherine: I know it sounds crazy, but she can smell cancer on people, she has said that she can be in an outside area in a crowd of people and actually smell the cancer on them. She is what's known as an empath, when she senses someone is very ill, no matter the diagnosis, she can feel a life of energy deficiency. She describes it as a grey fog that feels weak if she "tunes" into it. Cancer in particular, she says, smells of rotting meat.

The next week Katherine arrived for the session. We exchanged a few pleasant words and I then settled myself on the massage table. Katherine got to work. She started at my feet, slightly resting her hands on them.

After a few moments she said, "I don't smell cancer on you, you don't have cancer."

Without hesitation I believed her. I still clung to my hope that I was healthy. I don't know exactly how to explain it, other than something about my diagnosis just felt wrong to me. But what were my options? How could I possibly risk something more going wrong? I needed to trust the doctors, the results, and what was written on the charts. But still, something in my heart told me otherwise,

About an hour and a half into our session, Katherine explained that she would finish with some Reiki, an energy-therapy that uses life force to heal. She had me lie on the table face up with my eyes closed. She then began to hover her hands above my feet, using the heat from my body's energy and divine energy through her palms to transfer any healing that needed to be done.

I felt so relaxed. With my closed eyes, the most beautiful patterns of light began to emerge. Slowly, banners of red, yellow, orange, blue, purple—every color you could imagine—exploded like rushing waves of the ocean, the brilliance in the colors was one I have never seen before, it was incredible!

Katherine's reiki traveled through my entire body. A rush of warm, powerful energy traversed up and down my spine into every crevice of my body. As she hovered over my pelvic area, there came this surge of coolness. It was so powerful I had to ask her afterwards why the sudden temperature change. She said when coolness rushes through a certain area it usually represents fear. It is amazing how the colors flowed as she moved back and forth continually without a pause from my feet to my head.

At one point I opened my eyes, just a little, to see if Katherine was having a similar experience. Oddly, when I felt her hands moving back and forth above my body, she was actually still—hovering above my feet with her palms facing downward at me. I spoke to her.

"Kath, do you see that?"

She didn't answer. She was consumed totally by the moment itself, and the powerful experience she was creating directed by God. I closed my eyes and returned back to my colorful, heavenly world. Katherine stayed at my feet, though I continued to feel her healing power all over my body.

The session ended just as dusk was settling into my bedroom. Katherine rose from her spot at my feet, took a deep breath and made eye contact with me. She looked calm and happy. I asked what her assessment had been, and whether she thought I would be okay in light of what was ahead. She was peaceful and reassuring.

"Lu, I didn't smell or sense any cancer or disease...and I know that what you are experiencing is excruciating. And what you have ahead will be challenging, indeed a formidable obstacle..."

I watched as her expression changed from serious to hopeful. "But, you are on the very edge of something incredible, something life-changing, something huge is coming your way! I don't have many specifics, but I can feel that it's totally transformative."

Life Interrupted

My hysterectomy was scheduled as a three-night hospital visit. Unfortunately, it took thirteen long and painful days of a stay in a hospital that I prayed I would never have to return to. My stay was agonizing: six room changes, angry nurses, sleepless nights, and antibiotics that made me sick beyond belief. There were nights that I felt like I was going to die. Katherine was not exaggerating when she mentioned the "formidable obstacle."

One night, Pastor Larry came to visit; he was our main pastor at our non-denominational church we attended. He was like an older brother to me. His services had prompted my desire for a more spiritual relationship with God, one in which I have never had. Todd had arranged for Pastor Larry's visit; he was increasingly worried night after night when I could not be released from the hospital due to illness, possible infection, and other complications. I was relieved to see Larry. His warm-hearted smile gave him a soothing presence that grounded me. Though I was weak and feeling a bit sick, I clung to each word he spoke to me. He was reassuring and light hearted. He teased me about joining the Life Group, a bible study group that I kept procrastinating about joining. I wasn't sure if I wanted to share my life obstacles and feelings with people I didn't know and I was afraid of being vulnerable. Wasn't it ironic, though, that it took an emotional and grueling life experience to finally join a "Life Group"?

I assured Pastor Larry that I would attend as soon as I was released.

On the thirteenth day, I was finally well enough to be released. The doctor came into my room to dismiss me. Following protocol, he described that I should expect menopause symptoms: weight gain, possible depression, and night sweats. I couldn't use hormone therapy because it would create more estrogen, and therefore a greater chance for cancer. He painted a pretty bleak picture. With every negative comment he made I replied with a smile.

"I appreciate what you're telling me," I told him, "but no, that's not going to happen. In fact, I will do exactly the opposite of that you're describing."

I held dearly to my optimism. I laughed through the pain and the fear of the unknown. Though my body and my hormones were undergoing massive and permanent change, I sought humor in every moment. I decided that I wouldn't be a statistic and I would only come out better on the other end. Once I made up my mind, that is precisely what unfolded in my experience.

Post-surgery, I required six to eight weeks rest at home in order to heal. For someone who can't sit still that seemed like an eternity, but I was committed to my recovery and I wanted to do it right. After all, I had been cut wide open.

After several days at home, I started to get restless. As I lay in bed, I contemplated some ways to fill my time. On a whim, I asked my husband if he could find some paints and canvas at a nearby art store. Painting seemed like a relaxing activity that requires little movement, and I thought it might be therapeutic to do something creative in a time of discomfort and healing.

I never painted before and I didn't have many hobbies, but I welcomed the materials my husband brought me. He walked into my bedroom and set a paper bag on the bed beside me. I peered in. It was a case that opened up and inside was at least twenty-five different colors, dark to lighter shades. Just the sight of them cheered me up. He also leaned a large canvas against the wall for my first project.

I started painting. I watched the colors expel onto the canvas. I followed the soothing pattern of spirals with purple and green. It felt both relaxing and engaging. The colors were speaking to me and manifesting into lines and shapes.

One day, I stepped back from my project and decided it was beginning to look like a whimsical tree. I continued the spirals outward, the branches, the roots, but no leaves. It began to take on a life of its own. I was painting a tree as a symbol for the time in my life. For the pain, the surgery, and at that time the unforeseen lesson. I channeled all of my emotions, the fear, the hurt, the uncertainty, and even the humor into the work, and as I did, it set me free.

I laughed out loud when the piece revealed its jokes to me. Once I wrote the word menopause, I suddenly thought "Men-need-to-pause," ha! I wrote in on the painting in the branches of the tree with a set of little reading glasses above it. Women change during menopause, and we need space from our spouses sometimes. Men are often "fixers" but they would do better just pausing themselves!

From that point forward, I started to refer to it as "The Menopause Tree" and it made sense. This tree was just one in a forest of trees that represented my entire lifetime of growth. I thought about all the trees I had created throughout the course of my life. What an idea it was to paint them each in their own unique way.

Expressing life as growth—both painful and beautiful—felt therapeutic to me. To encapsulate each lesson and season in my life as a work of art caused me to look inward for meaning in a very deep way. And if you really think about it that is exactly what we are here to do. To learn through our mistakes, and to be imperfect in every way. What's the sense of life here on earth, other than to learn from our choices and mistakes! That is what makes us who we are, and through those experiences, good and bad, we eventually find our true purpose.

As I continued to learn more about myself, my creativity grew. My perspective on my own life changed. I considered all the chapters of my life and started painting "Chapter Trees" to visualize them. After the "Menopause Tree" was complete, I moved to an "Inspiration Tree" for women battling breast cancer. Then, a "Wedding Tree," a "Bambino Tree" for a new baby boy and a "Bambina" for a girl. I searched my life for new Chapter Trees and I did them for my family and friends. Through drawing, I felt a release of emotions that I had a hard time expressing. It allowed to me search deep within myself to answer all the unanswered question that life had thrown at me through many interruptions. Even if I didn't find the answers, I was closer to knowing my own truth. I owned all the trees, all the chapters, the questions and the interruptions. I painted them on canvas to finally set them free.

Though staying home and doing nothing seemed utterly unbearable, it revealed to me a precious gift. I learned to slow down, to take my time, and most importantly to look inward. When I made the conscious dive into myself, I found my creative voice speak from deep within. What started as painting quickly moved to ceramics and journaling. I admired the work I created, and felt surges of emotions kept deep inside of me come forth into my creative healing.

Life Interrupted

CONCLUSION

"It is a joy and delight to plant new seeds, for I know these seeds will become my new experiences."

A S I REFLECT on all that has happened to me, I remain hopeful. And hopefulness, joy, compassion, and peace are what continue to lead my life. It's a big difference than living a life based in fear.

I hope that in sharing my story, I have motivated to you

rewrite yours. We all have the power to become the creators of our own dreams. I hope that you will feel inspired to create big, beautiful, hopeful dreams, and chase them no matter what may interrupt you.

As I close these pages, I would like to acknowledge my loving husband of twenty-six years, Todd. He has always been there for me with optimism, kindness, and love—he is my rock. Todd encouraged me to follow through on my dreams of writing a book, and he taught me to keep going even when it was tough. These scars of my past still hurt when I recall them, no matter how much time has lapsed, and Todd reminded me to stay strong in spite of that. I am willing to revisit the pain countless times if it means just one women reading this will heal from my example.

If that's you, know that I'm here for you in spirit. I am rooting for you to get to the core of things, even if it is hard. Especially if it's hard! Know that using your voice is power. Buddha once said, "There are three things that cannot be long hidden: the sun, the moon, and the truth."

It's when we have the courage to seek our healing
then we can truly be free.

We all possess the same seeds as the apple—the same inner intelligence. Our minds and our bodies will always evolve to a higher truth, as long as we are free from the darkness of our past. Every day, I remind myself to live free from mine, and my life is one of peace and happiness as a result. I wake up grateful, and so should you. You should live the life you've always dreamed.

From the heart,

I AM ON A NEVER-ENDING JOURNEY OF DISCOVERY

If I were beginning to write about my spiritual journey, where would I start? What was it that sent me on my journey? Was it something I read or heard? In reality, my spiritual journey began before I took my first step in life. There is always an undeniable yearning of the created to connect wholly with the Creator.

When I went on an inner journey, I realized that the spirit of God was at the core of my being. My journey did not end with this discovery. Every day I have 24 hours to live, move, and be as God's love in expression. New and amazing realizations come to me as I continue to make progress on my never-ending journey of discovery

Put these things into practice; devote yourself to them, so that all may see your progress.
1 Timothy 4:15

ABOUT THE AUTHOR

Luann was born and raised in Milwaukee, Wisconsin. She spent eight years in Orange County, California working a variety of different jobs before returning to her roots.

She currently lives in West Palm Beach, Florida with her husband, Todd, and sons Austin and Nicholas.

Luann is an avid artist and spends time volunteering at the Kids Cancer Foundation teaching painting classes and spending time with the children and their families.

She also uses her artistic and design talents in the way of creating her own recipes, writing, painting, interior design and loves entertaining guests. She enjoys spending time outdoors kayaking, playing tennis, Pilates, and gardening.

www.lulublu.com

Made in the USA
Columbia, SC
17 November 2018